Thoughts on the Tabernacle

Thoughts on the Tabernacle

illustrated

J. Denham Smith

KREGEL PUBLICATIONS
Grand Rapids, Michigan 49501

Thoughts on the Tabernacle, by J. Denham Smith. Copyright © 1987 by Kregel Publications, a divsion of Kregel, Inc. All rights reserved.

Library of Congress Cataloging-in-Publication Data

Smith, J. Denham.
    Thoughts on the Tabernacle.

    Previously published as: Christ Unveiled, or, Thoughts on the Tabernacle.
    1. Tabernacle — Typology. 2. Bible. O.T. Exodus — Criticism, interpretation, etc. 3. Bible. N.T. Hebrews — Criticism, interpretation, etc.
I. Title

BS680.T32S65 1987   220.6'4   86-27631

ISBN 0-8254-3756-3

1 2 3 4 5 Printing/Year 91 90 89 88 87

Printed in the United States of America

Contents

6 Contents

Preface

I COULD have wished that it had fallen to the lot of some more able pen than mine to write a preface to these Meditations on the Tabernacle, which contain the latest words of ministry to us from our beloved friend, that tender, loving, honoured servant of the Lord, J. Denham Smith. They are his last utterances on earth, dictated from his dying bed, or, to speak more truly, from the gate of heaven; for of him it might be affirmed that the words of the Lord Jesus Christ were fulfilled—"He that believeth in Me shall never see death." But I have felt that the privilege of having my name connected with the final words of one so dear to myself, and so beloved and honoured in the church of God, was too great to be declined, even though feeling fully conscious of my inability to do justice to the subject of it.

These few words of preface are not, however, intended as a sketch of the life of our friend,

neither do they pretend to be even a record of
his abundant labours in his Master's service, nor to
treat at any length of the grace and sweetness of
his life.   Indeed, for those who had the privilege
of knowing him, no biography will be needed.
Always cheerful, always kind, full of sympathy
and of love unfeigned, his private life, as well as
his fifty years of public service, might be summed
up in the words of the apostle—he was an
"epistle of Christ, written in our hearts, known
and read of all men."

Filled as he was with solemn and exalted
thoughts about God, his ministry presented the
Godward as well as the manward aspect of the
Atonement, an element in the presentation of the
gospel the want of which is much felt in the
preaching of the present day.   He felt that it
was a solemn as well as a glorious thing to be
saved, and so he lived out the truths which he
taught; and those who had the privilege of
visiting him during his long and trying illness,
will testify that *he died in the power of the truths
in which he lived.*

I may say then that the object of this preface is
simply to state that the subjects treated of in this
book were the subjects of his closing meditations
on earth.   They were commenced a little before
the time of his long illness, and were taken down,

as they fell from his lips, by the members of his family, and were continued to be written from his dictation to within a few days of his departure.

Many parts of these meditations were dictated by him on awaking out of sleep, and some when he was very ill. One unfinished chapter has been completed from a former small work of his own. Other parts needed slight correction, but no material change has been made, as it was not only what he said, but the form in which his last words were uttered, that will be valued by those who knew him and loved him.

They will therefore be received as his last words of ministry to us ; and if at times there may be somewhat noticeable any lack of that vigour and clearness which characterized his previous writings, it is only what might naturally be expected from one suffering great bodily weakness and prostration. But nowhere in these pages will there be found any lack of communion with God ; on the contrary, there will be felt to be a manifest intensifying to his soul, even at the times of his greatest weakness and suffering, of the reality and preciousness of the truths which he loved to teach when in the full health and vigour of life. Indeed, it will be observed in many places through these chapters, that his utterances are more those of rapture than of exposition ; and he appears at

times rather to be speaking to himself and to
God than to his readers.

He rests from his labours, and his works do
follow him; and we may now think of him, in
the words of Dr. H. Bonar, who quickly followed
him into the presence-chamber of their common
Lord, as—

> " Alone and safe in the holy keeping
>   Of Him who holdeth the grave's cold key;
> We have laid him down for the blessed sleeping,
>   The quiet rest which His dear ones see."

And may we not add—

> " Oh, who would not covet so calm a dying?
>   Or who would not rest by the side of thee?"

This book forms an echo from the very gates
of the glory; for it was his last occupation,
concerning which he said—

> " Perhaps for His name,
>   Poor dust that I am,
> Some work I may finish—— "

It might be truly said of him "that, living or
dying, he was the Lord's." And if his last words
uttered and his last lessons lived on earth are
made a help to any of the wayfarers here, who
are still making their way to the goal which
he has reached, the object with which these
Thoughts have been published will have been
blessedly attained.

                                        F. C. BLAND

Preview
The Tree of Life

"I sat down under His shadow with great delight, and His fruit was sweet to my taste."—Song of Solomon 2:3

THE Tree of Life is Christ. For shadow there must be substance, and this Tree has many branches luxuriant of leaves with whole clusters of fruit on every bough. Passing my seventieth year, and for a time my strength being weakened by the way, I took for a luxuriant meditation this Tree of Life. I felt now that it was not preaching about its clusters, or pointing others to its fruit, which for more than fifty years I have done, but sitting down under it and plucking anew its fruit for my own soul. All the great truths conceivable are represented by it, as all the treasures of wisdom and knowledge, with the whole fulness of the Godhead bodily, are lodged in Christ. I have said, there are clusters on every bough. It is under these one sits with great delight.

The most ancient of all fruit is, that of all things

He is the Great First Cause. There are four "beginnings" in Scripture. "I write unto you, fathers, because ye have known Him that is from the beginning"—*i.e.* His own beginning here, theirs with Him, the beginning of Christianity. Secondly, "I was set up from everlasting, from the beginning, or ever the earth was." *I*, the Christ of God. Thirdly, "In the beginning was the Word, and the Word was with God, and the Word was God." So that He was before all other beginnings; in fact, was not merely *with* or *like*, but *was God*. I can imagine an infidel who denies the whole of Revelation, but I could never understand a Socinian who says he believes in Revelation and yet rejects the Godhead of Christ. The fourth is that with which Scripture commences the unfolding of its wondrous tale—"In the beginning God created the heaven and the earth." This is a bough of eternal duration and fruit of infinite sweetness. How read we? "In the beginning was the Word"—the *logos*, that which is the most simple expression of what it represents. The heavens are not a full expression of God. Christ is; "and the Word was with God." If we were to stop here a question might arise; but, "and the Word *was* God." Nothing could be more absolute, nothing more complete. What intense confidence we have in this truth, because

He is the Rock of Ages, the Rock of our salvation, beyond whose Will and Work there can be nothing.

The second fruit is Sovereignty; and here one great truth leads to another. Nothing is more commanding than sovereignty. Before creation had a beginning all BEING was in Him, and it depended on His own sovereign will whether any other beside Himself should exist. In the same way it was wholly dependent on Him whether, when man fell, there should be redemption, but His thought of redemption was eternal and unchanging. Redemption by His precious blood; we are not our own, we are bought with a price, hence the gift of eternal life, because having Him as our Redeemer, "this is life eternal, that they might know Thee the only true God, and Jesus Christ whom Thou hast sent." What a cluster is Ephesians i.—"Blessed with all spiritual blessings in heavenly places in Christ: according as He hath chosen us in Him before the foundation of the world . . . having predestinated us unto the adoption of children by Jesus Christ to Himself, according to the good pleasure of His will, to the praise of the glory of His grace, wherein He hath made us accepted in the Beloved. In whom we have redemption through His blood, the forgiveness of sins, according to the riches of

His grace." A heavenly inheritance, "sealed with that Holy Spirit of promise, which is the earnest of our inheritance until the redemption of the purchased possession." But, much as we know, it is only a taste compared with the eternal feast. Yet it is sweet, for surely having been redeemed is sweet, and the forgiveness of our sins, "in living or in dying," how sweet! "Absent from the body," we are to be "present with the Lord," living or dying, it is the Lord. And "I *sat* under His shadow."

Calm sabbatic rest—sitting down, no work, no toil, but repose, rest—as He said, "Come unto Me, and I will give you rest." Precious in life, and at the close of life, is this attitude of the soul. "I sat down under His shadow with great delight, and His fruit was sweet unto my taste." Many are the shadows in which blessed fruit is formed. We put in our hand among the enfolding leaves; it is all fruit—plentiful fruit, heavenly fruit. It is one thing to have fruit, and another to have the taste. How often does an invalid eat, but that is all; he has no taste; there is no sweetness, no delight. But here "taste, delight, sweetness," carry with them their own meaning to the heart of one who lives in health and life before God.

For example, how sweet is peace with God, and assurance of salvation and a justified state—

sanctification, righteousness, meetness for heaven, a title to eternal glory! These are the leaves that heal now, and on a vaster scale will heal whole nations by-and-by.

It is there under His shadow, when we look to Him, our faces are lightened and we are not ashamed; it is there, when we seek Him, He delivers us from all our fears; and it is there, when we cry to Him, He delivers us out of all our troubles. It is there also we interpret nature; its songs and its sighs, its major and minor keys. We know that the whole creation groaneth and travaileth in pain together until now; and we know how the creature shall be delivered from the bondage of corruption into the liberty of the glory of the children of God. The sun shineth—the fruits and the flowers, they are the remains of Eden; the storm, the hurricane, the malarious air, the devastating elements, they are the result of the Fall. Yet the storms and the hurricanes, the voice of the Creator, what are they but incentives when they awake that we should awake to praise the great Creator, whose voice is upon the waters, whose voice maketh the hinds to calve, and breaketh the cedars of Lebanon. It is on such an occasion that it is said, " in His temple every thing saith, Glory."

It was first seeing the Tree of Life that we saw

the gospel, and now it is sweet to our taste as at the first. The "whosoevers" were clustered with wonderful life-giving fruit, by which the dead could live. "God so loved the world, that He gave His only begotten Son, that *whosoever* believeth in Him should not perish, but have everlasting life." Again, "*Whosoever* will, let him take the water of life freely." And again, "*Whosoever* shall call upon the name of the Lord shall be saved." And yet again, "*Whosoever* drinketh of the water that I shall give him shall never thirst." It is in preaching this Tree that so many Christians become, as it were, converted again; not that they get into a higher truth, for the truth never was low, but they have got to be where they ought to have been at the first. And now, in sitting under this Shadow, the gospel looks down upon us with cheering eye, saying, "Behold the Lamb of God." In gazing at this Tree of Life we see all the great truths embodied in that most ancient and wondrous type—the tent of the congregation and the Tabernacle of God, to which now we are about to direct our inquiring and meditative minds.

1

Introduction

"My meditation of Him shall be sweet."—Psalm 104:34

THE great peculiarity of these Thoughts is, that they are practical and experimental, and especially adapted to the present day, unfolding, in words easily understood, the great plan of God's redeeming love.

God has made innumerable worlds. He created all those heavenly orbs which bespangle the bosom of immensity. We are told that when He made our world He made the stars also; and we read of principalities and powers and angels that have their estates. This little world of ours belonged to the great family of worlds; but as in every family there are diversities—one may be sick, and the thought of the family be concentrated on it; another may be rebellious, subject to no law, to no wish of the family, no wish of its head.

OUR LITTLE WORLD

was this. It became sick, and a rebel province amid the great universe of worlds; but as a father pitieth his one child that is sick, and yearns in compassion over the one rebellious son, so God still loved, and withdrew not His pity. On the contrary, He came down to the sick one, and determined on a *salvation* such as had never been seen. He so loved it, that He Himself expended on it no less a gift than His beloved Son, who died for its guilt. This He did that He might reclaim and enfold it in His heart of love. Christ died ; and by His death God is satisfied, the love of His heart is gratified. He now sends the message of it to all, brings it nigh to the sons of men. But man, alas ! for the most part rejects it. It is this marvellous plan of salvation that is so opened out to us, as a parable or a picture, in this wondrous structure of the tent of His divine dwelling in the wilderness.

THE TABERNACLE

is an ocular source of knowledge, bringing God and His ways very near to us, by means of gold and silver and other precious things most akin to His nature. Scarcely is it simple faith (though faith receives it), but a sight of the great leading truths and principles which are found in all other parts of the divine Word, affording, as it does, so wonderful an epitome of the Person, work, and offices of Christ, and showing so much

of the hidden man of the heart, and spotless
holiness of His life, that fresh light and enjoyment
are for ever attendant on its study. We know it
is typical, and this knowledge is not only steady-
ing but satisfying. There is a solemn tendency
to make types where they were never intended,
to place on them interpretations of our own
imaginings. To indulge in such is not only
presumptuous towards God, but misleading and
injurious to the souls of men. God is a jealous
God concerning every word of His. Moses not
only lost the land, but had his life forfeited by
changing one word : being told to *speak* to the
rock he *struck* it. Nothing is more responsible or
solemn than our dealings with divine truth. Where
there is a doubt as to how far the type may extend,
it is always safe to use the word " suggestively "
for a type or any truth that may suggest what may
not have been by God immediately intended. The
Rock has been stricken, and needs not to be
stricken again ; that is, Christ has died, and needs
never to die again ; but speaking to Him and receiving from Him, we find an endless and eternal
fulness of truth, a river of never-ceasing delight.
There is no limit, no finality, but an endless variety
and an eternal continuity in that for which Paul so
earnestly and definitely prays, " That I may know
Him, and the power of His resurrection, and the

fellowship of His sufferings, being made conform-
able unto His death; if by any means I might
attain unto the resurrection of" (from among) "the
dead."

The whole system of the Tabernacle is a hammer
to shatter every system of an infidel unbelief—fruit
of the haughtiness and enmity of man, which can
prove nothing but his own contemptible folly.

Wonderful reply is it ever to the dark assail-
ments of those truths and principles in these days,
which, as occasion offers, we shall show.

Never did the Word appear more as a rock of
certainty than now. This one can say, after more
than half a century preaching its blessed truths,
when not a long time can remain of life, and,
moreover, after an illness in which the border-land
of the eternal world was near; all the foundations
were seen by the eye of faith as infinitely safe,
infinitely sure, and infinitely sufficient to bear
the foot of faith all through.

For the Christian, Paul speaks of a day when
we were illuminated; this we had at our conversion : "If there is a moment of moral energy
in the history of a soul, it is the day of its quick-
ening." As at conversion we begin with sin, so
here .we learn what sin is. It has been said, "If
we do the least sin we ought to be broken-hearted
about it." This is true—oh, how true!—in the

light of God's holiness against it, and Christ's
sufferings for it; such as is seen in Psalm lxix.
and xxii. But if sin is seen, grace also reigns
through the sacrifice of Christ, and sin is put
away, not only sin, but sins. The priests were
always clean when they appeared before God.
" The pavement of His presence was never stained
by the foot that entered it." It has been the
experience of many that their

FIRST REAL LOOK INTO HEAVEN

—that heaven which is beyond all these lower
heavens, God's own *interior* heaven, was through
the knowledge of this wondrous type. They
have followed Christ from His sufferings to the
risen and ascended life of His glory at the right
hand of God. How blessed the first introduction of such things to the heart! What a type
that can disclose such secrets! " It is," says
another, "a divine library; you may take down
one volume from your shelf and read about *the
heavens*, in another volume you read of *man in
ruins;* take down a third and you read of *God
in grace*, and so on in wondrous, precious variety."
the sun . . . cometh " out of his chamber and re-
joiceth as a strong man to run a race." Many
of the stars, we are told, vary in their lustre.
They are seen to have become enlarged in their

dimensions, also more luminous. This may be from a nearer contact with other fountains of light. How nearer could we be to the very highest sources and fountains of light, as we go from altar to altar, from the holy to the holiest, and understand how the glory of God shines in the face of God's ascended and glorified Christ? It is thus we become fountains ourselves.

But how many there are who can say, that the first insight they got into the ritual and symbols of the Tabernacle was to them a *second* illumination, which they carry with them all the days of their life. May I not hope that eyes alighting on these pages may be lifted to see the rich, glorious heritage in divine truth, and the rich, glorious inheritance which is theirs in Christ, so simply and grandly unfolded to their view in this wondrous type.

These thoughts are thoughts of Christ, full of the gospel, but specially suited to the soul bent on the greater enjoyment of Christ. For me, in very quiet hours, they have formed a delightsome occupation. There is nothing truer than this, that our inner affections crave for expression ; as one has said—

> " How sweet, how pleasing sweet, is solitude !
> But grant me still a friend in my retreat
> Whom I can whisper, Solitude is sweet."

And another that, "Co-heirs cannot sit silent on their glories." This study is inexhaustible, as is the study of all God's works. The earth on which we live still has her secrets. The tiniest flower that grows, with its lovely pencillings of the divine hand, and sweet, refreshing odour, yields its unceasing delight. And lifting our eyes to the shoreless, illimitable universe, what millions have found the same who have gazed upon

> " Those countless stars, like golden dust,
>   That strew the skies at night,"

presenting, as the result, an endless harmony of voices, and an equally endless variety of impressions; some, gifted with the powers of admiration, observing them as God's best beauties and magnificence in His created works revealed to earth ; some dwelling on their mild nocturnal glory, worlds on worlds and vast systems of worlds, filling the mind with deep, irrepressible wonder ; some on their immense immeasurable distances ; and some again thinking pleasantly of them as of the many mansions of the Father's house. Numberless thus are their impressions. Here, in this revelation of the Tabernacle, is what goes beyond all worlds. Each lineament possesses some divine, wonderful theme of infinite meaning, filling the soul with the grandeur, the glory, and the infinite grace of the Infinite Himself. But none can claim that anything ever yet said by man has been final, or that nothing more remains to be told. It is the Christ of God who is so plainly seen, and He is a great deep; His ways are past finding out. Accordingly, the impressions derived have been many, and varied as many; no two minds, perhaps, have ever felt precisely alike. Neither the lessons learned, the admiration expressed, nor the devotions kindled, are in any two cases the same. It is this which makes fellowship in writing, as well as in speaking, so delightful. The result is a harmony of divine testimony, to be obtained in no other way. In eternity, through all its endless ages, it will doubtless be the same. The millions of the blood-bought redeemed, with the innumerable orders of angels, will see and know and feel beyond telling, all blessed and all varied, yet in perfect harmony one with another—

> " Ten thousand thousand are their tongues,
>   But all their joys are one,"

as the beautiful hymn of Dr. Watts says. Delightful are the recorded views on this subject. Not to speak of men ages ago, many others dear to the church of God naturally come to mind. A goodly array of these have seen the same Tabernacle, but returned from the sight, each one richly laden with results others may not have had. Thus was it with the prophets of old—Isaiah, Jeremiah, Daniel.

They all saw the same Christ, the one magnificent, mysterious, glorious Being, so prominent in prophecy, who was to come a Saviour and Deliverer into the world, and who was to fill heaven and earth with His praise; but the strains with which they rehearsed their hopes and joys, though nothing contradictory, were never the same. Do we see nothing grand or inspiriting in this? Glorious will it be thus with our redeemed minds through all eternity.

Nothing gives greater fulness and brightness to the divine Word, or our hope and confidence therein, than the study of the Tabernacle; only—and the condition is absolute—we must take Christ with us, and apply Him to each object we see. He is the true key to unlock each treasure, and we would suggest that our standpoint is not now the earth but heaven. The apostle tells us this, the wondrous patterns are no longer here, we look in vain for them. Other patterns will yet be given for the earth, but these are patterns of things now in the heavens. We first see the copy with our minds transferred to heaven, in order to discern that of which it is a copy. Either way—we may look first at the one and then at the other—always a pleasant look for faith, transferring the eye from things which are seen to the things that are not seen, and from the unseen things to the things which are seen.

Sweet treasury of divine art! From eternity, the pastime, as it were, of the divine mind, formulated by the divine hand. What a picture of His infinite grace and love! It is a marvellous memorial of Christ before Christianity, and among the former things of old by which God spoke concerning His Son. We would fain call it all to remembrance, saying here at the altar, "This is His death;" and in the courts, "This is His life after death;" for the blood of the altar is everywhere upon all the other vessels, even where God's eye, in His special dwelling-place in the holy of holies, is ever resting upon it.

Who that would know Christ before ever the prophets sung, or evangelists wrote, or apostles preached, may know Him here. It needs no fanciful interpretation. Happily there is a common understanding of it that gives rise to the sweet sense of fellowship with all those who have walked about this Zion where God had His throne and dwelling, or lingered amid its calm retreats and solemn resting-places, of which we shall delight to tell; indulging in their study of heavenly art in gold and silver and curtains of every hue and adorning of vesture, as seen on Him who walks there, now in robes of white, and now in garments for glory and beauty.

"Big with bright truths is every atom here."

Light unchanging! "Gold—gold—gold!" we exclaim with hushed voices as we enter. All is gold, and tells of the "inheritance incorruptible, and undefiled, and that fadeth not away." What a sweetness of mind each object lends! How calm their manifestations!

As we enter we think of Proverbs viii., "with Me," says Christ, are "durable riches." How blessed to see them in Him! Yes, all is sure, unchanging in Christ. Nothing is so elsewhere, especially to one who has been lying, as it were, on the border-land, anticipating all its multiform and multitudinous glories. What compared with these are millions of money! Health, youth, joys, pleasures, fame, love, friends, are not durable. Our most delectable things are not durable. Thus the bard—

> "Ah me, the affections of this life grow old
> And die, like spring-buds, in the pinching wind.
> Love, even the deepest, cannot last; at morn
> 'T is fair as light; ere even exhaled like the dew,
> Or, like a rainbow, buried in the cloud
> From which it rose, and upon which it hung.
> The dearest tie that ever knit two hearts,
> Each like the other, as two budding roses,
> Snaps, and the loved one passes out of sight;
> The brightest eyes are fading, and their sparkle
> Is vanishing amidst the mortal mist
> That wraps the globe, and darkens earthly homes."*

* "My Old Letters."—BONAR

Oh, vast is that which we enjoy outside these things of time! They are all in Christ; "with Me," He says.

Who would not write with such a theme? Angels would fain hold the pen; we need to be guided.

Much dreamy ethereality has mingled with the interpretations which not a few have given of Scripture, especially of its symbolical representations. But, as we have said, there is an all-admitted understanding of it, which gives no place for what is merely fanciful or ideal. Some might say, Why write? Why multiply the number of the records? Oh, the happiness of this study! how sweet its repose! The joy of many a spare and sparce moment at home and abroad, ever bringing Christ to a near view, reminding us of the quaint words of another—

> "O Jesus Lord! My Saviour Lord!
> Forgive me if I say,
> For very love, Thy sacred name
> A thousand times a day."

Surely that is why one might write. Concerning the High Priestly vesture, and the many details of the colourings, and the gold and the silver, &c., of the sanctuary; the thoughts might be my own or others. It matters little; we are debtors to one another. They are, I believe, in

faithful accord with the whole scope and canon
of Scripture. With confidence, therefore, can I
commend them to all as suited to this day
of neglect and denial of divine truth, and to
those moments when the soul is occupied simply
and only with the Lord. Of course anything
man can think or do must ever fall short of the
full truth. Some of the minuter details may
seem as if they had no direct meaning. But
He who never made a mistake in planting the
star in the heavens, or the flower on the earth,
had a perfect design in every pin and every thread
found in their allotted place. " The just shall live
by faith," what the eye sees now is Christ in
heaven. It is there we see the true Tabernacle,
the true Holiest, the secret place of the Most
High. Yes, it is there ; freed from the defilements
and distractions of earth, we breathe the air suited
to our divine nature. It is thus He brings us
nearer and yet nearer to His own heart. It is
there, with holiest confidence of faith, we meditate
on the strength of those foundations which God
in Christ has put under our feet. Moreover, it
is there in spirit we enjoy, through such a medium,
the deepest intimacies of our communion with
God, and the brightness of those prospects which,
as one with Christ, He has yet in store for us.
Oh, sweet it is thus to look away from ourselves,

and over and beyond the hilltops of time, as Moses on his Pisgah heights, with Christ and heaven, and the heaven of heavens all in view, where especially Christ appears for us the greater than Aaron, and where God is, in whose presence there is fulness of joy, at whose right hand there are pleasures for evermore! The effect morally is blessed.

> "For how the thought of God attracts
> And draws the heart from earth,
> And sickens it of passing shows
> And dissipating mirth!"

But why do I preface thus? Why linger at the threshold, when so much has to be seen? and yet one word of praise and adoration. For this we need an angel's lyre, a seraph's tongue.

Once sweetly did they sing on seeing the true Tabernacle descend—"God manifest in the flesh"—"Glory to God in the highest, peace on earth, good will towards men."

> "Oh, my God,
> I thank Thee for the inestimable gift
> Of Thy Son Jesus Christ; that miracle
> Of counsel and design, as well as love.
> The only argument that could explain,
> Resolve, and vindicate Thy ways to men,
> And reconcile the hearts of men to Thee.
> Christ is the Causeway which, unflung to earth,
> Had left the gulf impassable betwixt
> Creator and created. Thus I die (live)
> A meek believer in the name of Jesus.

Through Him I feel no terror for my sins.
Vast as they are, they harass me no more.
Their price is paid in full ; and I may call
God, whom I've outraged, my Saviour, my Friend."*

When entering on any scene of interest, we like to know something of what it is : indeed, descriptions beforehand will be studied over and over again. The pleasure of anticipation will be in proportion as the hope of the realization will be bright.

Ere we enter this scene, extending from the outer court to inside the veil, we can say there is not a single thing in which a child of God is not interested ; not one. The loops and pins, the mere goats' hair and badgers' skin, as well as the massive and almost priceless gold, are all of deepest meaning and greatest value. Who can look at the priest in his magnificent attire and not think of a glorified High Priest in heaven ? Who can see the blood poured out at the altar and not think of the cross of Christ ? Who can see the innermost place of the glory and not think of heaven and God—the secret place of the Most High, the shadow of the Almighty ; His feathers, under which, by faith, we trust ? Oh, it is endless, the discoveries we shall make again and again of God and His ways, of Christ and salvation, as,

* *Anastasia.*

with the divine description in our hearts, we tread
these several courts of the Lord, which He set up
to manifest His Son! It was our own Gentile
Apostle to whom was given the setting forth its
distinctive glories, or rather the distinctive glories
of Him of whom the Tabernacle itself, its wondrous
furniture and garniture, its offerings and its priesthood, were the varied and multiplied shadows; "and
I," may a child of God led by Him say, "among
the many have had my own holy and happy times
with the same. God has spoken to me from out
of His holy dwelling-place. I have seen the Man
of sorrows in His sufferings the same, and arrayed
in His garments for glory, and for beauty or
honour, as the word is. I have washed me at the
laver, and heard of my sin at the altar; and his
sins shall be forgiven him. I have entered the
holiest by the blood of the atoning sacrifice, and
with open face have beheld the glory of the Lord.
The beauteous cherubim, with sweet human face
divine, and the glory beneath their wings, have
told me their wondrous tale. How impossible for
anyone else to know just what I have felt, or
describe the impressions made by what I have
seen!" But just as we like to hear one another
upon a theme in which all are interested, so do
I delight to record my own.

God well pourtrays His own work. The Scrip-

ture is so lucid, and presents everything so plainly,
that every object of itself seems to stand out
visibly to the eye.   These truths· are a near
display of Christ.   They are a near manifestation of God ; they are a mirror too of ourselves,
our sins, our desert, our present salvation, and our
coming glory.   They are a guide to holiness,
happiness, service, sanctification, and complete
redemption.   Who does not remember the first
time when these types were seen to be full of
Christ ?   "What," I said in my first days of
their knowledge, "*it* shall be accepted for him ?"
What ? Prayers ? Repentance ? Gifts ? Service ?
Nothing of the sort, but Aaron having a golden
mitre on his head, with "Holiness unto the Lord"
inscribed upon it.   "It," God says, whereupon
faith sees Christ.   The Jewish mother may be
attending to her babe ; the Jew attending to the
striking or lifting of his tent—nay, the whole
tented army may have been asleep. No matter.
"It," Aaron, who through the blood was "holiness
to the Lord" for them.   "It," Christ,· will be
accepted for them. What joy ! what liberty ! what
peace !   And oh, gratitude and praise unspeakable
when first this vast little word was understood in
the soul.

This is true of what we have now, but the
Tabernacle is full of the "notices and attractions"

of divine and heavenly things to come. They bear our minds away into that heaven and those heavenly things of which they are the patterns. And in proportion as they do this we are made "strangers and pilgrims" here. They tell of heavenly glories, a heavenly Man, a glorious High Priest in heaven, of heaven itself, and of ourselves through the blood of Christ admitted there. But can we read these notices of what heaven is, that it is to be ours by-and-by and for ever, and as we read, not wish our hearts joy that it is so? Can we but count ourselves happy in having such prospects as these? As the miser can bear the scorn of the world without, in the thought of his treasures of gold, cannot we, in the hope of our joy in heaven, live above the earth and all its poor habitudes and ways?

Oh, what is not this to the soul that knows it? "The Song" (chap. vii. 9) speaks of the best wine that goeth down sweetly (or straightly), causing the lips of those that are asleep (or are old) to speak. Surely no truth can be sweeter or better than that which we see here. And surely, again, none can see it, however previously asleep, or old, and infirm even, but must speak. Where, if not in the holiest place, could the heart be more filled; and it is out of the fulness of the heart that the mouth speaks. It is for us that the blood is there,

and the mercy-seat is there, and the glory too—all
for us.   One knowing it all as the fruit of the love
and grace of God, and of the eternal, dying love
of Christ, can say, "I am my Beloved's."   I may
say of the Queen, " She is my beloved sovereign ;"
but I could not say, " I am her beloved."   Yet this
is what the youngest or latest born of the children
of God can say of the blessed One who loves us,
surveying the grand colossal heights of divine
purposes in Ephesians i.—those heights which form
the vast boundaries of our holy Christianity : " In
whom we have redemption," and in whom we have
" the forgiveness of sins."   Having also believed, we
are " sealed with that Holy Spirit of promise."   As
another has said, "What are these glorious purposes
but the beating out of the gold of Psalm cxxxix.,
' How precious also are Thy thoughts unto me, O
God! how great is the sum of them ' ? "   It is
embedded, as it were, in these.   He can say, " I
am my Beloved's."   It has been said of the
Christian, as seen in Ephesians i.—seated in Christ,
walking in Christ, standing in Christ—that " he is
a Christ-enclosed person."   This is true ; and so,
in the holy of holies, the one who is there is a
God-enclosed person.   All around, above, below,
all divine.   It is all God in Christ ; and the
believing sinner, through the blood which is there,
sees himself as loved with an everlasting love,

saved with an everlasting salvation, "accepted in the Beloved."

And now what need we more but to remember the words of Paul the apostle, which so forcibly show the connection there is between the doctrine and the life we now should live. "Always bearing about in the body the dying of the Lord Jesus, that"—that what? why that as the natural result —"the life also of Jesus might be made manifest in our mortal flesh." It is of no use to talk of doctrine, to admit the value of the atoning death, unless the outcome in our lives is, living the life such as Christ lived. The life to be manifested is not only His life in resurrection, but His life on earth, His walk with God, His obedience to the will of God, His philanthropy, the love He had for us, the compassion He felt for the poor, the sick, the sorrowing. A life all unselfish and full of blessing for others, is the life natural to our belief in His Person and the atoning value of His death.

General View of the Tabernacle

The Tabernacle with Its Coverings Rolled Back

2

The Tabernacle

"I will set My tabernacle among you."—Leviticus 26:11

THE Tabernacle forms a distinct revelation within the revelation God has given of Himself in His Word. It is a representation which the eye can see of His beloved Son, and a programme of His work of saving grace. We may note first

ITS CHARACTER.

The term Tabernacle is from a word signifying "to dwell." Hence, "let them make Me a sanctuary, that I may dwell among them." The only obstacle to our belief of such words is the marvel that seizes us at the greatness of the disparity between the One who is to dwell and those with whom He seeks His dwelling. Wondrous thought, God dwelling with man! Illimitable grace, founded, as we must believe, according to all His great character—observable to the universe of an infinite perfection! Psalm xci. speaks of our dwelling with Him—" He that dwelleth in the secret place

of the Most High shall abide under the shadow
of the Almighty." And again, "He shall cover
thee with His feathers, and under His wings shalt
thou trust." But *here* it is God dwelling with us.
The all-embracing heavens declare His glory, and
such conduct as His having made a point through
all eternity—of coming here and dwelling first in
His tent of the congregation with a wandering,
sinful people, and the deeper mystery in the Man
Christ Jesus, and now in the Church, which is the
habitation of God through the Spirit—shows His
illimitable grace. Beginning with Genesis, and
looking on to the eternal dwelling in the new
heavens and new earth, we thus find God's
delight is with men. And all between these two
great beginnings is a testimony to the love that
would have it so—a divine harmony of voices,
telling us of this all through the ages, from the
angels' song over Bethlehem to the far end, amid
the glories of the new heavens and the new earth,
in which His tabernacle will be with men.

Speaking in general terms the Tabernacle is a
grand *similitude*. It has been said—

"Things seen are mightier than things heard;"

and an old writer has remarked, "Similitudes
ennoble the circle of our thoughts and desires, and
possess more power than words. They not only

present wisdom to us, but they make it to abide."
"In some," says Tyndale, "there is the star-light
of Christ, in some the broad light of day." Their
use is common with the divine Being. Faith
cometh by hearing, and hearing by the Word
of God; but God has given these for the eye,
that the eye may affect the mind. Christ is the
Author of all we see in the heavens and the earth,
and whilst here often took a parable or picture
from nature as from His own book. Now it
was the lovely tiny flower directing the eye to
its pencilled beauty; as He said, "Consider the
lilies . . . how they grow; they toil not, neither
do they spin." And now it was the birds of
the air, which neither have storehouse nor barn;
"Behold the fowls of the air." Sometimes it was
a pastoral scene: "I know my sheep." And
again it was the bread before Him: "I am the
Bread of Life." What are Luke xv. and John
vi. but parables (pictures) for the eye—the lost
son, and the lost sheep; nor was the great Teacher
alone in this. David, Zechariah, Isaiah, and all
the prophets received and taught wondrous truth
through objects presented to the eye. Daniel's
image unmistakably taught of the great world-
powers which would fill all time. The Tabernacle
is a symbol, not from nature, but art. Its object
was more fully to bring us into a nearer view of

what God is, and of what redemption is. The earliest worshippers knew something of God's way of life. It was seen in the garden, and in Abel's offering. Abraham owned he could not meet with God excepting through a sacrifice. The Passover, and the offerings by Moses in the wilderness, all told of the same. But here was a wondrous enlargement upon it all: it formed an epoch in the divine ways. It was a sweet, yea timely, epoch in the garden when the glorious gospel strains first fell from the Divine lips, showing that where sin abounded, grace did much more abound. It was a further epoch when, in virtue of a "slain lamb," God redeemed Israel out of Egypt. But the Tabernacle was the fullest exposition, a more elaborate symbol than any before. It showed in a most striking way how God could meet the confessing sinner; *i.e.*, be just, and the Justifier of the ungodly. A large amount of traditional knowledge must have nourished the faith of the chosen of God; and here was a parable of the whole work of human recovery—in fact, the gospel made manifest and easy to the believing mind. It is a voice which, from over the long interval of thousands of years, still tells us simply and fully of the death, resurrection, and ascension of Christ. It is interesting to think how similitudes will not cease with the present, but will reappear in the millennial days of earth's glory. The river issuing from the Temple will be a delightful image of the water of life proceeding from the throne of God and of the Lamb. The several feasts will tell of the far wilderness, and other days. Pleasant to know how in all ages the eyes of the redeemed have been directed towards the same Christ. The types were not like man's exhibitions, which served their little day, and then died in forgetfulness. Kings and bards and prophets have perpetuated their memory; millions of minds have sought to penetrate their meaning; angelic beings desire to look into them. Especially is the Tabernacle God's symbolical, I might say prophetical, portraiture of His beloved Son. He who in the far ages saw the Tabernacle, saw Christ; and he who saw Christ, with more or less intelligence, grasped this symbol. It is a foreshadowing of God's Christ, of God and of His delight in His redeemed people. It is a type also of His Church, which, one with Christ, is the habitation of God through the Spirit. Moreover, of all believers who are spoken of as "living stones, built up a spiritual house, an holy priesthood, to offer up spiritual sacrifices, acceptable to God by Jesus Christ." Hence it is symbolical of every child of God. Wonderful words! "We are a sanctuary of the living God; even as God said, I will dwell in them, and walk in them; and I will be their God, and they shall be My people."

Thus he who knows the sanctuary will know God —the one only true God, whom to know is life eternal. Therefore it is we linger over and over and over again on each detail, never tiring in our visits to the courts of the Lord's house so bright with His presence, and never tiring of seeing Christ —now His person, now His rank, His work, and now His glory; and being one with Him, we see our share in all the riches of the glory of the inheritance which everywhere in this treasury of love are laid open to our view. Nor are we the less moved by seeing His humiliation and suffering. Oh, vast repository is our blessed Christ of all the treasures of wisdom and knowledge; yea, of all the good things, now and for ever, which God has for us in His gospel! Who that desires divine knowledge let him come; he who would be saved let him come. In the epistles we transfer the eye from Christ symbolized to

CHRIST PLAINLY STATED.

In Colossians i. we have the most wonderful sayings; it gives the sublimest programme conceivable of both creation and redemption. Let everyone read and see. Could any language in heaven or on earth ever excel it? How sublime the Person! Possessing, as we have said, all *Being* in Himself, it was wholly within His own option that any other than Himself should ever exist. But in the exercise of His sovereignty He determined on the existence of the two great departments of creation—the earthly and the heavenly. Sin entered into both. There are "angels, who kept not their first estate, reserved in everlasting chains, under darkness unto the judgment of the great day." Man also sinned, and fell under death and hell. He, whose creation the earth was, of His own will determined for us a work of salvation, and bears the name of "the Firstborn of every creature." Not that He was the first to be born : certainly not. By emphasis, He, who is before all things, is truly first—eternal. His other ascribed name is even more wonderful—"the Firstborn from the dead." Was He so called because He was first to die, and to rise again ? Certainly not. But by dying He settled the question of death for sin, and hell the doom for sin ; and by His resurrection from the dead showed how vain was death. He rose the beginning of a new creation, and Head of the body (the Church), that in all things He might have the pre-eminence. In this sublime, glorious programme there are the two compartments—the things in heaven, and things on earth. The one answering to all those wonderful transactions on the great day of atonement in the outer court of the Tabernacle; and the other to all those glorious things of every hue and value, together with the rest and peace, in the Holy and Most Holy Places. He reconciles all things unto Himself —the things that are in heaven. And "you that were sometime alienated . . . . by wicked works, yet now hath He reconciled in the body of His flesh through death, to present you holy and unblameable and unreproveable in His sight." Note, not by the Spirit, as some suppose, or through His life, as others, but through *death*. Naught else could effect so glorious a work as that a sinner could be counted holy and unblameable in the Divine sight. None need ever doubt

ITS ORIGIN,

but must believe it originated alone with God. We are strangely told by some that men devised it centuries after Christ, fitting each part to the salient events of His life. Truly it seems a satire on the theology of the present day, that heads of learning and professed teachers of advanced religious thought, as it is called, deny the inspiration of the books in which the Tabernacle is found. Why not deny the whole Scriptures? for they are throughout the unfolding of what the Tabernacle typically and prophetically is. More-

over, Moses himself is denied. Why not deny
Christ too, for Christ spake of Moses? And how
is the Epistle to the Hebrews to be disposed of?
Are we to doubt Paul? Nothing shows the inspiration and foreknowledge of the Word, and of
its remarkable foretelling supernatural power, than
the way in which, near two thousand years ago,
warnings were given to aid us in these last days.
In Paul's day he could say, "For I know this, that
after my departing shall grievous wolves enter in
among you, not sparing the flock. Also of *your
own selves*" (*i.e.* not professed infidels or unbelievers,
but men who professed the truth) "shall men
arise, speaking perverse things, to draw away disciples after them." (See also 1 Timothy iv. 1, 2;
Colossians ii. 8; 2 Timothy iii. 1, 2.)

No; He who alone can foretell the future—and
only God can do this—was its exclusive Author.
From ages before Christ appeared it pointed to
Him and His works, as though His Voice had
audibly said, "This is My beloved Son, in whom
I am well pleased;" "Behold the Lamb of God,
which taketh away the sin of the world." It tells
of the essential quality of eternal knowledge—
how all is laid out before it, from the beginning
to the end of everything that is. Besides its
construction, like the Bible itself—one part so
perfectly agreeing with the other, the light of one

so grandly in unison with all—its being no longer simple prophecy, but obvious history, stamps it as the design of such a mind. It is said men doubt this, even the learned. It is the learned who have ever led off in any new doubt that he who was a liar from the beginning had suggested.

But they are excellent men. "Excellent men!" *Never mind*, rather than deny God, let God be true and every man a liar. Looking at its super-natural, nay, prophetical character, for it is a perfect prophecy, I would say, "Bold infidelity, turn pale and die!" for who but God could foretell the future? As we have intimated,

ITS ANTIQUITY

also is in question. God gave nothing to be ques-tioned, but to be received; yet man in the pride of his heart will question. All history can tell of its antiquity. We are told it was fabricated some hundred years after the Lord's death. The Jew would like to have said this, but his whole history was against it. Besides, what would he do with Moses? The whole literally miraculous preserva-tion of his Bible, even every jot and tittle, is a mighty hammer to break in pieces such a delusion. The Jew failing, it was reserved for the so-called Gentile Christian, but he too is confronted with Moses. If he deny Moses he may deny the Lord, for the Lord spake of Moses. No works are so

old as the books of Moses, none so great, giving
us the oldest history or record of creation itself.
How commanding! How without apology, or
prelude, or introduction of any kind, we read " In
the beginning God created the heaven and the
earth." Uncertainty sits on the efforts of man's
restless reason in the present day. He would
fain find out how the world came to be in some
or any other way, but cannot. There are books
written six hundred years after Moses, but what
are they? poor, puerile things compared with the
incomparable one! If it were only for its literary
perfectness, in comparison with them, I should be
prepared to believe the Bible inspired. Where is
another book to compare with it? " The extreme
antiquity of Genesis," says the learned author of
Hours with the Bible, "gives it a surpassing value.
It stands at the head of the literature of the world
—the oldest in existence. From the opening to
the close it has an aim which sets it above all
uninspired productions. It is an introduction to
the history of the dealings of God with man,
which forms the ruling theme of the whole Scriptures. It throws," he adds, "a mysterious grandeur
over it, when we look at it in relation to Scripture.
As a whole, it is the porch of the great temple of
revelation, leading step by step to the disclosure
of Jesus Christ as Lord and Head of the new

kingdom of God, restored by Him among men after having been lost in Eden." No step in the earlier world was greater in its disclosure thus than the rites and symbols and priestly arrangements of the Tabernacle. Its record lies in Scripture as an unchanging, unchangeable rock of divine truth. No ; years have rolled into centuries, and centuries into millenniums of years, since it was set up by Moses. Aged truly it is, but not decrepit ; old, and yet young in power still to help and bless. Life, light, and joy, that were in the heart of God from all eternity, are the glorious elements contained therein. More fresh in the hearts of believers, call it old or young, in these darkening days are the truths it tells than with multitudes in the church in the wilderness, who in in those far-off ages had their tents immediately around it. None can contemplate the Tabernacle without specially considering

ITS MATERIALS.

As we have said, they were all selected by God Himself. Sweetly familiar He seems to become with us in this His chosen employ, telling just what was in His heart. It has been said of man, the most capable and skilled—

> " Dwells within the soul of every artist
>   More than all his efforts could express ;
> And he knows his best remains unuttered,
>   Sighing at what we call his best."

God had no sighing thus. His best gift, in symbol with an infinite simplicity and fulness, He places before our eyes, saying, "This is My beloved Son, in whom I am well pleased." God said to Moses, having only Moses between Himself and His redeemed offspring, "Speak unto the children of Israel, that they bring Me an offering" —a word signifying to "*lift up*," as if God would specially delight to see what was brought. And what were the offerings? "Gold and silver"— things that come nearest to His Divine nature— " brass, and blue, and purple, and scarlet, and fine linen, and goats' hair, and rams' skins dyed red, and badgers' skins, and shittim wood, oil for the light, spices for anointing oil, and for sweet incense, onyx stones, and stones to be set in the ephod, and in the breastplate." These were samples of the materials. We may fairly say no suns or stars throughout illimitable space were ever to God what these were. *They*, the former, set forth His creative power; *these*, His redeeming love. The former were the works of His hands; *these* told of the death and resurrection of His Son. However minute or humble the type, it was a vessel containing infinite treasure, image of Him " In whom are hid all the treasures of wisdom and knowledge." This is a large theme, and will be amplified more and more as we proceed. Those

who gave the materials were to offer them willingly.
Some were rich, and could bring gold and silver ;
and some were poor, and could only bring the
goats' hair. But the small, as well as the large,
represented Christ. And whence this gold and
silver ? Marvellous were the riches which the
people brought out of Egypt, reminding us how
Christ's inheritance has been taken up out of the
hand of the enemy. Doubtless the gold and silver
taken from the Egyptians by the 600,000 men,
besides women and children—shall we say, at
least a million and a half of people ?—were in-
calculable. On leaving Egypt, and as slaves having
nothing, they had specially *asked*, not borrowed
(see R.V.), jewels of silver, and jewels of gold ;
and the Egyptians, who had seen the awful
prodigies in Egypt, the death of their firstborn,
their dust turned into vermin, their rivers into
blood, their days into thick darkness, and longing
that Israel should go, willingly and abundantly
gave. As to the rest, it may seem a small thing,
a mere nothing, to bring a little modicum of goats'
hair taken, it may be, from the open desert, its
bushes, or its brambles, yet it was just as precious
to God as the most costly gifts of gold and silver.
It may seem a small thing for faith to touch but
the hem of Christ's garment, but it was really
Christ her faith touched. "Virtue," He said, "is

gone out of Me." None can believe in Christ
and not be saved. Remarkable too

ITS APPEARANCE.

It was twofold—first, its *outward aspect;* and,
secondly, its *inward glory.* These strikingly
showed what Christ in His rejection would be
as He appeared to men. Singular no one of the
evangelists ever gives a single instance of what
His Person was. We note too what His Church
is, as seen and disowned by the world. Any
stranger looking at the Tabernacle from without
must have marvelled. It was not an ordinary
building in which to dwell, nor an ordinary tent
in which a traveller may rest. Gorgeous and
costly as it really was within, to outward appearance it was unattractive, reminding us that though
Christ was truly divine, when men saw Him there
was no beauty in Him that they should desire
Him. Abundant as it was, there was no gold to be
seen from without. In His humiliation and shame
He did not reveal Himself to the world, as neither
does He now. He was as a root out of a dry
ground, than which nothing could be less attractive.
He had no form or comeliness, was "despised and
rejected of men ; a Man of sorrows, and acquainted
with grief." The external coverings were certainly
remarkable, about which much might be said.
They were a sure preservative for the precious

riches within—goats' hair curtains, loops also for these, and also rams' skins dyed red, and a further covering of badgers' skins. What the appearance was we can easily imagine: nothing rich, nothing costly, nothing attractive, no adorning. Why was it thus? The glory was there, but not manifested to the world. Just as there is a hiding of Christ now. "The world," He says, "seeth Me no more;" but, He adds, we are to be manifested. The covering will be taken off at His coming. There was no covering on the Solomon edifice suited to the dispensation it represented; it was all glorious. Josephus says of it, "The exterior part of the edifice wanted nothing that could strike either the eye or the mind. Overlaid throughout with massive gold, it reflected the sunrise—so fiery a lustre that those who constrained themselves to look upon it were compelled to avert their eyes, as from the solar rays. To strangers approaching, it seemed from a distance like a mountain covered with snow; for in those parts not overlaid with gold the building was of purest white. On its summit were fixed sharp golden spikes, to prevent the birds from settling and polluting the roof." All this as a type in its place is beautiful, giving glimpses of what He was on the holy Mount, when He, Moses, and Elias were seen glorified together.

But note further, there was no such outward splendour with our Tabernacle. The glory was all within; underneath the curtains were boards of shittim wood standing up, for which sockets of silver were provided. Moreover, bars of shittim wood were for the strengthening of the boards, these, their rings and bars, were overlaid with gold. The altars in the Holy and the Most Holy Places were opulent in gold. The cherubim and the mercy-seat, and the lamp with its sevenfold light, were all of pure gold—inward riches hidden from the eye of man.

The curtains, which were of fine twined linen of snow-white perfectness, told of Christ, who was perfect before all worlds, and could not be less so when on earth in humiliation—"a Man of sorrows, and acquainted with grief." The curtains were bound together by "loops of blue." A holy and a heavenly bond unites Christ and all His members —eternally and unchangeably one; in Him dwelt all the fulness of the Godhead bodily. "In whom are hid all the treasures of wisdom and knowledge." "No man hath seen God at any time; the only begotten Son, which is in the bosom of the Father, He hath declared Him." "Eye hath not seen, nor ear heard, neither have entered into the" (dark, natural) "heart of man, the things which God hath prepared for them that love Him. But God hath revealed them unto us by His Spirit . . . yea, the deep things of God."

These will all come before us in the Holy and Most Holy Places. Let us specially note that in all these

GOD WAS HIS OWN ARTIFICER,

outward or inward. Moses indeed may collate or build, but only according to the pattern delivered in the mount ; reminding us how we may minister, but only according to God's own written Word. Nothing do men need to learn more in these days than that no fancies or attainments of our own will do instead of the plain, unadulterated word of God. Each material was an object of specific choice, as each member of the mystical body of Christ was chosen in Him before the foundation of the world. "In Thy Book," says Christ, "all My members were written, which in continuance were fashioned, when as yet there was none of them ;" they were all foreknown as complete in Him. The Tabernacle thus is a rehearsal of what occupied Him from all eternity : especially did it foreshadow the excellency and glory of Christ as heavenly and divine, and the glory of His redeemed people who are as He is : all this was done as never before.

When was gold so used ? or the pure, snow-white

linen, foreshadowing our fitness for the divine presence and the glory in that city of gold? It has been well said, "That which was by command of God wrought in man's labour is there the nature of the place." His delights are with the sons of men, and there will His Tabernacle be. There too, besides the gold, are the precious stones, which on earth were varied displays of God's nature: they will there shine in permanent glory, and adorn the foundations of the city. That on which men walked, as in the desert, instead of bringing danger of defilement, is itself righteousness and holiness—gold transparent as glass. The one scene of the secret place of the Most High is the type of the other. In both there is no need of created light, neither light of sun or stars, the Lord God and the Lamb are the light thereof. Delightful is it to follow the inspired penmen as they depict these symbols, and this vision wherein the Incarnate Godhead is set forth. A voice comes —oh, may the heart hear it!—from each line and word, telling of His purposes in our redemption and salvation through His shed blood.

In association with the Tabernacle were

THE SACRIFICES.

Their blood was always and everywhere seen. God's requirement was, that the book of the law, the people, the several altars, and the Tabernacle itself should be sprinkled with blood. For without shedding of blood there could be no remission of sins. How this bears upon the errors so rife in the present day we shall see. It was in virtue of the blood shed as an atonement for sin that Israel could know and enjoy God. The case is thus stated : "Though redeemed, they carried with them into the wilderness an evil heart of unbelief, prone to depart from the living God;" though saved, they had a depraved nature still cleaving to them, hence the sin-offerings and trespass-offerings were for the conscience. The other offerings were for communion with God ; such as the peace, the meat, and burnt-offering sacrifices—offerings, as we may say, for the heart.

Moreover, the high priest was to appear for them before God ; provision was made for all sin, even our inmost sin and uncleanness. These may have been discernible only to the eye of God ; and if He were to dwell in the midst of them, all their uncleannesses, and all their transgressions in all their sins, must be dealt with according to His own estimate of what they were. Singular theology is it that ignores this. Truly well it is for the child of God to be clear about it, for every discovery he makes of the impurity of indwelling sin is sure to disturb his rest, and

mar his fellowship with God until he learns that
what may be a discovery to him is no new discovery to God. Without knowing this he is sure
to be caught in one of two snares ; he will either
have superficial ideas of what sin is, or his conscience so defiled by its pollution as to be shut
out from the light and joy of the divine presence ;
but if we apprehend and appropriate the priesthood
of Christ to meet all our infirmity and impurity,
as we have rested on His sacrifices to meet all
our guilt, we shall be able to write ourselves the
" chief of sinners," and at the same time nestle
our weary souls on the very bosom of our Father
and God ; knowing that the more closely we draw
near, the more trustful we are in the presence of
God. All this will be seen with greater clearness
as we contemplate Aaron in his office—the many
offerings which form the constant ritual of the
people. But in these our thoughts where shall
we end ? There never will be an end. And
what gives charm to it all is, that He who is
here in symbol is our own Saviour, the blessed
and beloved of our souls. Speaking so *of* Thee,
how sweet to rest awhile and speak a little *to*
Thee ! Loving, blessed Lord, how sweet to call
Thee ours ; and to tell our hearts of Thee !
Such unfoldings of our salvation and redemption
as seen in Thee, and such love and grace of the

Father: to know Thee is to know the Father. Precious words: "he that hath seen Me hath seen the Father;" and again, "I go unto the Father;" and again, "that where I am, there ye may be also." Blessed transforming task to know and see the Father in the glass of the Son, and to know and see the Son in the glass of this divine symbol. The effect is holiness; separation from self, and from sins, and from this present evil world. Concerning

ITS PEOPLE.

They were exclusively Israel. Paul the apostle says, "to whom pertaineth the adoption." In God's sovereignty He chose them as His own. This choice may not seem to wear the aspect of an eternal one as that spoken of the Church, which is said to be chosen in Him before the times eternal. (R.V.) The one has its course specially connected with this time-state, the other ranges beyond, before, and after all time. Extraordinary was God's interest in Israel; it roots far back in the days of Abraham, whom He called His friend, as He says of Him so sweetly, "Abraham, My friend;" and Jacob, the poor pilgrim-man, whom He named "Prince with God." To know Israel is to have a wondrous display of the character of God, which had a deeper forecasting

than we have any conception of; for in this world
a people of magnificent form and fashion will
yet be seen with all the attire and opulence of
the supreme people of the world—in fact, the
princes who, with God, will reign over the earth
and possess it.

The Tabernacle is called the tent of the congregation; congregation roots from the same word
as gregarious, signifying a flock, which Israel was,
whom He led as such, and who were taught to
say, "The Lord is my Shepherd." From out of
Abraham and Jacob He gathered them into this.
Now to them belonged the Tabernacle specially,
and in their midst did God place it. He was
thus by day and by night journeying and resting.
Can we picture it? amid unbounded space in a
desert a people encamped, as if at rest by day
with their watch-fire by night, having this tent,
God dwelling in their midst, as He had said,
"let them make Me a sanctuary." What a
supremacy of perfection! What a sovereignty
of care! What a directness and tenderness of
observation! We might imagine the scene—God
in His dwelling, and this congregation arranged
in beauteous order around. And we can imagine
how a solitary Israelite—at night amid storm
or gloom, or having the thought of an enemy,
could, folding back his curtain, turn his enquiring

eye to the calm, lucid light of the cloud, and say, "All is right, all is safe, the Lord is there, God is in the midst of us." Peacefully he may resume his rest, with no fear, no terror, no thought of ill. And this, notwithstanding by day and by night all around was one vast solitude. Far and away, stretching in the blue distance, was there only the desert, with the world dead concerning it, as now it is dead to Christ—"waste" as to man and "howling" as to beasts of prey. But God was His people's Guide, Protector, and Provider. Oh, what dependence! We see more than a million of people with no home, no habitation, and no food that they could obtain from the wilderness; moreover, at times they had no water. What an image is this of our own dependence upon God, of our own lack of resources, and also of what God is to us! for all our springs are in Him; it is He alone who can supply all our need. Image truly of His ever-watchful care!

I once asked an aged child of God, "Are you never afraid, as you are left lonely—a widow, with no one to protect you?" "Ah, no!" was her reply, "I never knew that Word as I know it now—'The Lord is thy Keeper: the Lord is thy shade upon thy right hand.' No, not lonely, especially at night I resign myself to sleep in the restful feeling that He is my Protector."

Said another, "I seldom go to sleep without turning my mind from bolts and bars and police, about which I used to think so much, to rest in His promise—'I am with thee,' and 'I will never leave thee nor forsake thee.' No; 'The Lord is my Shepherd, I shall not want.'"

Say in this wilderness what enemy *could* touch the cloud of His presence? What storm could bend it? No; God, who was always there, looked out with ever-guardian love from its midst upon His redeemed people. How blessed it all is! Truly "The eyes of the Lord are upon the righteous, and His ears are open unto their cry." As in the past so now, "He that keepeth Israel shall neither slumber nor sleep." Need I say what volumes, thoughts upon thoughts, may flow to our minds from the contemplation of all this? Blessed Lord, "sanctify us through Thy truth: Thy word is truth."

Historically the Jew and Jerusalem as to all that has occurred are well known. It is in knowing them we see the love of God, know the righteousness and grace of God, and become so intimate with Him.

But now as to Israel, God showed Abraham much that finds place in the Tabernacle—the sacrifices he offered, the altars he built—and especially the way He would lead Israel as in a furnace, with the animals slain in sacrifice carefully placed on either side, reminding, as subsequently He did in the Holy and Most Holy Place, how the only way to be righteously where God was must be by way of death. Abraham's seed was four hundred years in bondage in Egypt, answering to the furnace; they were redeemed out of it, answering to the sacrifices; they had the wilderness journey where was the Tabernacle; on reaching the land were the supreme people of the world; but by departure from God became what they now are, yet only for a time. There are three words of the prophet which indicate their whole history. Glancing at the *past*, God says, "Be ye not as your fathers." For the *present* he prays, "how long wilt Thou not have mercy on Jerusalem?" "I am returned to Jerusalem with mercies," foretells the *future*. The words indicate how their history is full of vicissitude. But God has been, and is, the same; the Alps, the Andes, or the Apennines may be rooted up, "the mountains shall depart, and the hills be removed; but My kindness shall not depart from thee, neither shall the covenant of My peace be removed, saith the Lord that hath mercy on thee."

This feature of the divine attitude is everywhere seen. From the days of Abraham to the days of heaven on earth He is unchanging towards Israel.

In the wilderness the pillar of cloud never left
them; even when they sinned, and had to be turned
back into the desert forty years, He went back
with them—true to His word, "I will never leave
thee nor forsake thee;" in their weakest times He
could say, "My Spirit remaineth among you." In
the day of Christ's rejection it was, "How often
would I have gathered thy children together."
And now, while in unbelief, under dispersion,
and robbed of their "ancestral territory," He is
the same, teaching them to say, "Wherefore should
the heathen say, Where is now their God?" This
as to the past and present. But as to the future,
high distinction and grandeur are before them,
God will have returned to Jerusalem. The symbol
in Zechariah i. spreads itself over more than two
thousand years of the past, present, and future;
the entire prophecy is but the enlargement of it.
Notwithstanding God dwelling in their midst, the
fathers failed; "unto whom the former prophets
have cried, saying, Thus saith the Lord of hosts,
Turn ye from your evil doings; but they did not
hearken unto Me." This is obviously a looking
back upon the past. The prayer of the prophet
Zechariah relates to the present: "O Lord of hosts,
how long wilt Thou not have mercy on Jerusalem
and on the cities of Judah, against which Thou
hast had indignation these threescore and ten

years ?"—a term typical of the greater and longer
indignation which now rests on them in their lost
and ruined condition.   As to their intermediate
position, who can read such words as Lamentations
ii. without seeing that no language could ever go
beyond its most true and touching description ?
Who can doubt *inspiration*, or that the literary
marvel of the blessed Word tells of that inspiration ?   Read verses 9–12, and tears may well fill
our eyes.   But first read the prophet's prophecy,
or rather history, closing with the Babylonian
chains of the young king; its record supplies
warning to our own souls as to how they ever
slight the faithful love of God and of Christ,
which we see is a love jealous of our own.

But behind all the dark cloud is the bright
shining of a glory ready to reappear.   Verse 16
is the unveiling of a glorious future : "Thus saith
the Lord ; I am returned to Jerusalem with
mercies : My house shall be built in it. . . . The
Lord shall yet comfort Zion, and shall yet choose
Jerusalem."   Yes, as surely as the sins of the
fathers, and the evil consequences that followed,
are all patent to the observer of history, so with
such promises as Isaiah lx., which opens up this
glorious future—theirs and ours.   They all wait
their fulfilment in positive history, and blessings
inconceivable yet to come.   Thus " the gifts and

calling of God are without repentance ;" He will never change ; His mind is according to His promise. That promise was not made conditional on their goodness, else whence would blessing come ? but unconditional to Abraham. The root of the olive tree of Romans xi. (symbol of their whole history) is not Israel, but Abraham, to whom God said, "To thee will I give it"—*i.e.* their land—"and to thy seed for ever." There was no condition, no covenant which Abraham had to keep, or which Israel had to keep, as there is none with us. The gift was absolute—that one land of this earth, which God afterwards called His own land ("Immanuel's land"); the only spot on earth which He ever thus called His own He gave to them ; a land extending from the river Euphrates, the river of Egypt, and from Lebanon, unto the great and wide sea. No possession of the land as yet has ever answered to this first promise; they occupied only in part.

Moreover, that was only for a little while, but God had said *"for ever."* They were driven out for their disobedience; they will return, according to the original promise, God giving a true repentance and a divinely-wrought obedience. For the present, Israel is "cast off." Other branches have been growing on the olive tree, of which Abraham is the root. But if these continue not in His goodness (which Christendom and the Church have not), they too, as to their being corporately owned by God, will be cut off.

In the absence of Israel, God has been gathering to Himself the Church in this dispensation. This being done, He will return to them again with mercies, these mercies constituting the long-promised millennium, in which all nations will call the Redeemer blessed, and to accomplish which there must come "the Deliverer." The times of the Gentiles reach from the days of Nebuchadnezzar to the time of the antichrist, whom He will destroy with the brightness of His coming. He will come the Hope of Israel, and in Him will be the fulfilment of all the promises relating to the glory of this earth made first to the fathers—Abraham, Isaac, and Jacob—and afterwards so plentifully repeated to the bards and seers, the kings and prophets, whose writings for the most part fill up the whole of the Old Testament. It is the crowns, as seen in our symbol, so brilliant and so beautiful in the Holy and most Holy Places, on the altars and on Aaron's brow, that show this, in all of which we are deeply interested.

Paul the apostle tells us how Israel came into their present melancholy history. Besides past ages of grievous iniquity "they stumbled at this stumbling-stone, as it is written, Behold, I lay

in Sion a stumbling-stone and rock of offence :
and whosoever believeth on Him shall not be
ashamed ;" they stumbled at His lowly appearance, and the sorrows as seen in the altar of
suffering; they stumbled at His person—they
could not accept a carpenter's son ; they stumbled at His doctrine—they rejected righteousness
by faith in Him, and sought it only in works.
Hence now, as Isaiah says, though their seed
become as numerous as the sand of the sea,
only a remnant believing in Him should be saved.
It is well to know this, to have taken this little
glance at a people who, by emphasis, were the
people of the Tabernacle, and whom God made
supreme as to their interest in it beyond all other
people of the earth. Besides, God is the same
unchanging, patient, loving One to us, else how
can we understand our own dispensation ? How
adjust our labours among men, or regulate our
prayers ?

Obvious is it that those who never read, or
who neglect prophecy, can never know their
Bible, but are ignorant of what God will yet do.
This prophecy, what is it ? It is God's mirror
wherein He has presented Himself, and His
doings, His plans, and His purposes. It is that
in which He has shown us the future of time
and eternity ; and this He has done that we

may have full sympathy with Him as One who treats us not as servants, but as friends. And who but God could know the end from the beginning?

> "All after thoughts belong to man,
>   With all the doubts that hang around us here;
>   To God pertains the eternal forethought and pure light
>   That knows no shadow of a shade; to Him
>   All space, all time, are ever, ever clear.
>   Himself the present, and Himself the future,
>   Himself the first and last—the All in All."*

Now such are the people to whom God thus committed Himself in dwelling among them; and no knowledge of the Tabernacle can be complete without a knowledge of them. Let us pray for the peace of Jerusalem; for "they shall prosper that love thee."

---

* HORATIUS BONAR.

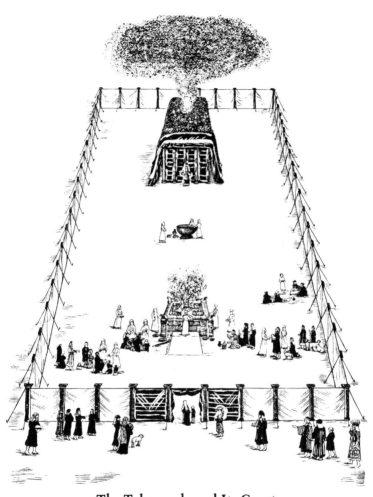

The Tabernacle and Its Court

3

The Court of Entrance

"And he reared up the court round about the tabernacle and the altar, and set up the hanging of the court gate. So Moses finished the work. Then a cloud covered the tent of the congregation, and the glory of the Lord filled the tabernacle."—Exodus 40:33, 34

THERE is nothing so infinitely momentous as the knowledge of the way of a sinner's access to God. Life and death, heaven and hell, all will be as that way is or is not known. We cannot say of it as we say of the thread of life—

> " My God, on what a *slender* thread
> Hang everlasting things."

No; it is the mightiest part of that great whole by which God can save the lost, making the very guiltiest to be the righteousness of God in Christ.

Hence it is of infinite moment to have it all through the truth explained to the soul. The outer Court was intended specially to show this way of access.

As we look around upon the Court, it is as if we saw inscribed upon it, " I am the Way, and

the Truth, and the Life: no man cometh unto
the Father, but by Me;" and "Him that cometh
to Me I will in no wise cast out." What makes
the place of such immense value are two special
objects—the altar and the laver, which we shall
more fully consider presently.

The entrance consisted of curtains of white,
blue, purple, and scarlet. These all were not only
for security, but for excellence, and to be admired
by the eye of him who, coming with his sacrifice,
would be filled with assured hope. As to their
construction, they reached some eight feet from
the ground, so that no wanton eyes could look
over them, or mere passer-by conceive of the
heavenly mysteries within.

The colours were wrought as beautiful embroidery into the purest white; white denoting
God's character, His holiness and righteousness;
also the blue, scarlet, and purple, indicating the
heavenliness of Christ as Man, the earthly glory
He will yet have, the reign and kingdom which
will be His. This work of embroidery God gave
for a profusion of uses; it was in the veil which
separated the Holy from the Most Holy, and in
the hangings and curtains of the tabernacle itself.
One thing only was absent—the cherubim were
not in the hangings of the way of entrance.
None need ask, Why these colours? Why the

pure snowy-white, the blue, the scarlet, the
purple? They all tell of great truths to be
known inside the Holy Places, and made good
in the sufferings of Christ, and the glory to
follow.

There were pillars for the hangings. They were
not fixtures as were the foundations of Solomon's
Temple; they were so erected that they could
be removed. Israel, as yet, had no settled rest;
they were redeemed, but not in the land; they
had still to journey.

The glorious Temple described by Ezekiel, and
which is yet to adorn the "mountain of the Lord"
in the latter day, has a wall surrounding it of
strong and solid dimensions, as if it rooted in
the earth, indicating a settled state of things in
the time of the earth's glory, suited to the establishment of the Messiah's kingdom. That will
have no temporary fence; no mere curtain to
be folded up for journeying, but durable and
unchanging, in accordance with the promise,
"of His kingdom there shall be no end."

Suggestively here, what answers to our own
brief life is the easy dissolving and removing
of the whole, so that the place that knew us
knows us no more. Yes, so soon could it be
taken down, so soon may the earthly house
of our tabernacle be dissolved. This bodily frame

is but as dust ; yea, fragile as the grass or flower of the field, which to-day is, and to-morrow is cut down, and withered. Psalm xc. says, "Thou turnest man to dust." (R. V.) "The days of our years are threescore years and ten, or even by reason of strength fourscore years ; yet is their strength (or pride) but labour and sorrow;" *i.e.*, the strength, not it would seem of the mere remnant only from threescore and ten to fourscore years, as generally supposed, but of the whole of our brief life from infancy to the grave ; "for it is soon gone, and we fly away." No sooner the dawn than the close comes. Sweet to contemplate our *building* of God ; "an house not made with hands," (not even as the Temples of Solomon and Ezekiel which, however glorious, are of the earth), but "eternal in the heavens."

Besides the pillars there were the sockets. These were brass—inconsumable, no fire could melt them ; they remind us how Christ could endure fires of divine wrath, and the contradiction of sinners against Himself. The fillets were of silver, made out of the redemption money. We are redeemed, not with silver and gold, but with the precious blood of Christ ; therefore we are not our own, but "bought with a price"—goods, alas! often withheld from their true Owner by Christians who have never been wholly surrendered to God. Oh,

what thoughts may naturally well up in the
believing and discerning mind as suggested by
this! Gracious Lord, we would bow before Thee
here in praise and prayer. Of old, Lord, Thou
hast made the heavens and the earth ; Thou didst
desire this habitation for Thyself. How blessed
that we may meet Thee here! it is here we
see Thee, as if Thou hadst specially appeared
to meet and receive the sinner who has received
Thee, and who has come out from the world
" drawn by love that knows no measure," the love
of Christ constraining him. It is here we have
found the new and living way, first to Thyself
(the sacrifice), and then to God, the only true and
living God. And it is here we see where " mercy
and truth are met together, righteousness and
peace have kissed each other." Thus in prayer-
fulness and praise, Lord Jesus, we enter here.

It is interesting to think of the offerer. He
comes from the camp just as the sinner, on being
awakened, comes from the world to where God, on
the ground of his offering, can meet him in peace.
He brings his lamb, as we will suppose, as a sin-
offering, for there were many offerings. Silently
and solemnly he leads his lamb, or with dove
in hand he uses for himself, if we may so say,
the sacrifice offered on the day of atonement
outside the camp. This is an image of how God

can meet man for blessing through the sprinkled blood. With what tenderness of mind would the offerer look upon his victim, innocent of guilt, unoffending and submissive! touching image of Him who "was brought as a lamb to the slaughter, and as a sheep before her shearers is dumb, so He openeth not His mouth." Notably the sheep is almost the only animal who makes no resistance to the uplifted instrument of death. Solemn is the transaction: besides bringing the offering, the offerer himself had to strike the animal with the sore blow of death; or if his offering were a dove or young pigeon, to wring off its head. All this would be felt of deep moment and real, in proportion as the offerer knew his need before God. If any remorse on the soul, God's promise respecting it would be his relief: he himself may not die, the sacrifice alone being destroyed. He laid his hands on it when it was dying, and fell, as some say, on his face to the ground when he saw it bleeding to death, feeling as if the death were his own; he could say, "Alas! that is my desert." Like Galatians ii., he feels as if "crucified with Christ." Not that the sinner is crucified, yet because he casts himself upon Christ and His sufferings, and sees Christ in his place, and as if one with Him he says, "I am crucified with Christ." He grieves that his sins had been the cause, but

it is not the grief which saves, just as it is not the
sickness that saves the sick. "Misery for sin,"
said Juan de Valdés in the sixteenth century,
"bears the same relation to Christ which sickness
does to the medicine." It leads to the medicine,
and misery for sin finds its solace only in Christ.
Supposing a sufferer now under remorse for sin
felt he had committed through a long life all
the sins ascribed to Israel in the wilderness,
and to each individual in the Word whose down-
falls are recorded; supposing, like Job with his
corruption, he could take the potsherd, as it were,
and scrape himself of his iniquity, what then?
Repent more? Carry still the load of the guilt?
Ah, no! the gospel is, that all our sins were laid on
Christ, and all the value of His death is reckoned
to us; He first provides righteousness, and then
reckons it to us; "The just shall live by faith."

I like what a martyr of the dark peninsula
in the fourteenth century said* in his *Confession of
a Sinner:* "In order that the devil shall have
no claim against me, nor slander against my
righteousness—the righteousness of God in Christ;
in order that the wrong and irreverency perpetrated
against the majesty of the divine law may be
wholly pardoned; in order that I may have greater
pledges of what Christ has done for me, and of

* The Spanish Constantine Ponce de la Fluente.

what Christ is to me; in order that the weight
of obligation might lead me, O Lord, to serve
Thee, might give wings to my soul to seek Thee,
Thou hast been pleased to die for me an infamous
and cruel death, delivered up to unjust judges to
be tortured and dishonoured in the sight of the
world, all in discharge of my obligation, all to
make it understood how much Thou hadst my
restoration at heart, by the price which it cost
Thee, and which Thou didst so willingly offer
for it. The devil has no longer any ground or
just pretension to accuse me, nor the world to
captivate me, nor the flesh to enslave me, for Thou
hast conquered everything. Thou hast died, in
order that I might find them vanquished. The
sacrifice of Thy blood made me free." This is so,
God has only one way of relief for the sinner.
The clothing of the first pair in the garden, Abel's
offering, Abraham's sacrifice on Mount Moriah, the
victims slain on Jewish altars, all tell the same,
that "without shedding of blood is no remission."
We cannot view the Tabernacle apart from the
sacrifices. Blessed way God planned, by which
He could be loving and gracious to man.

Diversified was the state of mind of the offerers.
Sometimes a sense of newly-committed sin, filling
the soul with its anguish, led to the appointed
offering; sometimes a sense of mercy or favour

bestowed, called for praise and thanksgiving, such
as blessedly we too know on the recurrence of
special deliverances.   It has been always so with
the family of faith.   How interesting to think of
Noah just out of the ark, with such a deliverance
from the death he saw before him on the old world,
whose inhabitants had all perished.   How happy
to see him with his ascending offering—an offering
of sweet savour unto God—and for God to receive,
and of true delight and unspeakable relief of soul
for him to offer.   The same with Abraham ; note
how his several altars told of his sense of being a
sinner needing a sacrifice for sin ; and how, when
remarkable mercies came, or remarkable promises
were made, he built his altar, and offered his offering anew to the Lord.   In like manner Jacob ;
those altars of his told the chief passages in his
life, his sorrows and his joys.   David, overwhelmed
with a sense of deliverance from judgment which
he himself deserved (seventy thousand of his
people having been slain by the Lord, concerning
whom he said, " But these sheep, what have they
done ? ") offered his thousands of offerings, indicating the greatness and intensity of his feeling.
Then Solomon, on the Temple being dedicated,
offered sacrifices more than could be told ; and
Hezekiah in a similar way.   We are apt to think of
such as Abraham as being simply worshippers ;

but indeed they knew they were sinners—poor sinners dependent on the mercy of God. And we too, do we not feel we have the heart which all these acts of devotedness indicate? Are we not the subjects of surprising mercy? Have we never had some overwhelming deliverance from sorrow or trial, that the memory of it even is more than we can tell? Oh, my soul, blessed are those meltings of heart before the Lord which He delights to see, those praises which He delights to hear! Beauteous Tabernacle! wondrous guidance and comfort have we thus in all its many rites, wherein God is merciful and man blessed; it is because of this we love to go from altar to altar, and from one sacrifice to another, beholding how

THE JUST LIVE BY FAITH.

Who that wants an increase of Christ in his soul, let him again and again traverse the whole ground extending from outside the camp to the far innermost scene of the Most Holy Place. Outside the camp, on the great day of atonement, once a year was sin put away; this was a transaction between the priest and God, or, in the antitype, between Christ and God. It showed God in Christ putting away sin by Christ enduring its tremendous penalty. Then, next from the camp, an offerer might be seen leading his sacrifice along to the place of death—availing himself

of the sacrifice made, shall I say? at the cross,
presenting the Christ slain for him outside the
camp. He has come to the altar, where alone
God could, so to speak, come out to meet him.
Passing the laver for cleansing, which we shall
describe, we reach the Holy and Most Holy Places;
there sin and suffering come not; but instead of
these, the holiest rest and greatest peace, together
with the most glorious symbols of the riches of
God's grace and glory yet to be revealed.

It was always on the ground of sacrifice that
God could accept man; the same will be seen
in a further age, as shown in the description of
the Temple. Sacrifices are on either side of the
entrance into it. " The dividing portions of the
victims," says the author of the *Englishman's Bible*,
" are seen placed on the tables on either side, and
hung upon the hooks a hand broad, on the right
hand and on the left, with the pathway between
them," giving wondrous significancy to the words
of the apostle in Hebrews x. 19, 20, 22—" Having
therefore, brethren, boldness to enter into the
holiest by the blood of Jesus, by a new and
living way " (literally, by a newly-slain and living
way; namely, by the death and resurrection of
Jesus) " through the veil, that is to say, His
flesh; let us draw near." Thus what was sym-
bolised by the rent veil of the Temple is presented

in a far more graphic and striking manner to
the eye by the divided flesh of the newly-slain
victim through the midst of which the priest
entered when he went into the sanctuary of
God. On the tables were laid the instruments
by which the sacrifices were slain. So the print
of the nails in His hands and His feet, and the
mark of the spear in His side, were shown by
the risen Christ to His disciples when He appeared
in their midst ; and the Lamb in the midst of the
Throne appears as a Lamb that had been slain,
bearing even in His glorified Body the memorial
of His sufferings on Calvary's cross. How beautifully does one scripture form an agreement with
another on this ! Voices of truth, how they blend !
The burning lamp, for example, in the days of
Abraham was seen making its way with the offerings laid out on either side, so that the lamp in
its passage was definitely between them.

Will you ever forget when, first awakened, and
wanting assurance, such words as " Whosoever will
may come," and " Him that cometh to Me I will
in no wise cast out " ? or will you ever forget
when, upon reading Leviticus i., the words greeted
you, " *It* " (the offering Christ, and not your feelings, or your repentance, or your faith) " shall
be accepted for him " ? God accepted Abel on
the ground of his offering.

The Altar of Burnt Offering or Brazen Altar

4

The Altar

"Thou shalt make an altar of shittim wood, five cubits long, and five cubits broad; the altar shall be foursquare; and the height thereof shall be three cubits. And thou shalt make the horns of it upon the four corners thereof: his horns shall be of the same: and thou shalt overlay it with brass. And thou shalt make his pans to receive his ashes, and his shovels, and his basins, and his fleshhooks, and his firepans: all the vessels thereof thou shalt make of brass. And thou shalt make for it a grate of network of brass; and upon the net shalt thou make four brazen rings in the four corners thereof. And thou shalt put it under the compass of the altar beneath, that the net may be even to the midst of the altar. And thou shalt make staves for the altar, staves of shittim wood, and overlay them with brass. And the staves shall be put into the rings, and the staves shall be upon the two sides of the altar, to bear it. Hollow with boards shalt thou make it: as it was shewed thee in the mount, so shall they make it."—Exodus 27:1-8

THE great feature all along this entrance line of things, from the victim slain outside the camp to the transactions at the door of the Tabernacle up to the Altar, is suffering. Who can tell the amount of suffering through all Israel's history ? Death, death, death marked this form of their ritual from one age to another ; but the sufferings were expiatory, substitutionary, atoning. Not that they themselves were atoning—that to which they pointed was. From childhood we have known the sweet explanatory hymn of Dr. Watts. What thousands have loved it and died in the faith of its truth! He sings—

> " Not all the blood of beasts,
>   On Jewish altars slain,
> Could give the guilty conscience peace,
>   Or wash away the stain.
>
> " But Christ, the heavenly Lamb,
>   Takes all our sins away ;
> A sacrifice of nobler name,
>   And richer blood than they.
>
> " My faith would lay her hand
>   On that dear head of Thine,
> While like a penitent I stand,
>   And there confess my sin.
>
> " My soul looks back to see
>   The burden Thou didst bear,
> While hanging on the cursed tree,
>   And knows her guilt was there.
>
> " Believing, we rejoice
>   To see the curse remove ;
> We bless the Lamb with cheerful voice,
>   And sing His bleeding love."

The Tabernacle at its Altar was the scene of perpetual death. Will anyone tell us why it is so? An innocent lamb slain every morning and every evening, the dove, the ox, the sheep, all in wonderful succession—multitudinous animals, one might say, brought to suffer, to bleed, to groan, to die; how inconceivable, if there were no great reason why God should institute this. Did He delight in inflicting sorrow and death? Did He desire man's heartlessness in sacrificing these innocent animals for nothing? Ah, no! it all has a true and wonderful meaning. Since the days of Cain and Abel the whole race of man has been divided into two; the one the Abel line, the other the Cain. The offering that Abel made was accepted of God; it owned sin, it owned salvation, and it owned faith in the revelation of these made to his soul by God; and all true believers on earth have done the same. They are the children, so to speak, of Abel; and by this, their faith, are separated from the Cain line, the difference being as wide as the poles, one pole from another; for as to Cain, who killed his brother, God had said to him, "A fugitive and a vagabond shalt thou be." Nothing humbled or deterred by this awful sentence, Cain, instead of being drawn in solemn contrition *to* God, voluntarily went out *from* the presence of God, as much as to say he did not want God or His directions. And as to his being a vagabond, he was too independent, and too religious for this; for Cain had an altar; but it owned no sin, no death for sin. From that to this, every human being born into the world is of the line of Abel or Cain—of Christ or of the world; there is nothing intermediate; every living man will in the issue be found on one side or the other. What a decisive course was the life of the blessed Abel, and what an honourable and a long-lived biography; for being dead, after the long interval of the ages, he "yet speaketh," or is yet spoken of. On the other hand pleasure, self-indulgence, so-called Cain-life ends, as it commenced, in enmity to God. There was no harm in the city or the music, &c.; but it indicated how determinately Cain was bent on making the best of this world independently of God—*Atheoi*, without God, and without hope in the world. Nor does their history end here; Abel, a star of the first magnitude, will gleam for ever in the light of God's special and eternal commendation, whereas "the candle of the wicked shall be put out;" that is, all their so-called joy and mimic pleasure will die with their death, but not so themselves. " The wicked shall be turned into hell, and all the nations that forget God."

The writer and the reader will be wise clearly to understand on which line he traverses; the one eventuates in life eternal, and the other in death eternal.

Let us now come for a little to what by

emphasis is The Altar. It is called the Altar as Christ is called *the Christ.* Every detail is of deepest importance, He alone can do the work.

> " Should the whole Church in flames arise,
>   Offered as one burnt sacrifice
>   The sinner's smallest debt to pay,
>   They could not, Lord, Thine honour share,
>   With Thee the awful justice bear,
>   Or bear one single sin away."

Bearing the "justice" shows why it is called

THE BRAZEN ALTAR.

Brass shows endurance; no silver or gold could endure the flaming fire. When Christ died, He could endure the sufferings, and when in the coming fiery judgments on the world, He will tread down the wicked, it will be with "feet like unto fine brass." A profusion of brass was in this Altar; it was everywhere upon the horns of the Altar; the grate and network were of brass; the rings at the four corners were brass; the pillars at the entrance rested on brass; any substance, such as gold or silver, would have been weak as water.

The sin-offering was consumed outside the camp once a year; but here the fire was always burning, and the blood always shed. What does it say? What but that Christ alone could endure as He did when the fires of God were kindled upon Him against sin? The brazen Altar thus plainly showed that "without shedding of blood is no remission."

Hence it is from this Altar, and looking at it from the long ages of the past, that instinctively our eyes turn to Calvary; were there no Calvary, no death of Christ, we should be at a loss for the meaning of it all. As *the cross* sustains our hope, so it is *the Person* that sustains the cross. Christ's personal glory is the sustainment of the cross; if He were less than God manifest in the flesh, all He did was no more than water spilt upon the ground. It is because of this He is able to proclaim Himself, "The Lord, the Lord God, merciful and gracious, long-suffering, and abundant in goodness and truth, keeping mercy for thousands, forgiving iniquity, and transgression, and sin;" sin the awful root, the evil received into our nature at the fall; transgression a going beyond, or sin in its evil action, and iniquity the fruit. Oh, what fountains of consolation to the sinful, transgressing, iniquitous ones who have fled for refuge to the hope set before them! The keeping mercy for thousands shows an infinite store ever ready for the thousands that need it; whilst He can "by no means *clear* the guilty," though He can, having died for them, *save* the guilty.

Who could number the cattle from a thousand hills, through long generations, which were slain on this Altar? Who could imagine their aggregate of woe? How great the number of the victims, those in the outer court, those outside the camp. We read regarding the court of Solomon, "The scene presented in this splendid court, where Solomon stood, must have left an impression never to be forgotten by those who witnessed it. Victims had been there sacrificed that could not be told for multitude. The polished floors were flooded with blood. The white robes of the priests, the glittering gates, the altar, were besprinkled and dyed in the same crimson stream; and the brazen scaffold on which Solomon stood to bless the people, seems raised on a battle-field where death had reigned. The God who is 'full of compassion,' by whom the death of a little sparrow is seen and noticed, cannot take pleasure in the slaughter of His creatures. Why then this scene of blood? we would ask again; for it is the solution of this which gives so tremendous and demolishing a blow to the so-called more liberal views of sin and death in the present day. In that awful hour in which the great Anti-type died, the curse rose from this earth, and spread itself in impenetrable darkness over that holy devoted Head, and the fire of righteous judgment leaped from heaven, and consumed the sacrifice, even as in the day of Solomon's dedication, before the eyes of Solomon and assembled Israel. This, to say the least, is matter of Jewish history, as well as of divine record. We ask the man who says he holds to the Bible, and yet rejects a sin-atoning sacrifice, how he accounts for this? how he reconciles it to his mind that it was *God* who directed it; yea, claimed it to be done? How was it He would not allow His creatures to approach Him but on the ground these sacrifices made? To be at rest concerning sin he must account for it. Hence we boldly say that the Socinian, and all those who deny the doctrine of sin and of atonement by the death of Christ, would never have had such an Altar as this; they would have no such sign of woe or shedding of blood. We commend this to them as a problem to be solved, in which their eternity of happiness or of woe is involved. Precious is it to faith, but revolting to reason: revolting indeed too would these sacrifices be to God, were it not for the great ends in view.

This denial is in keeping with the whole monstrous system—the system of denial—so growing in this our day. The Godhead of Christ, the atonement for sin by the death of Christ, justification through the blood of Christ, are all vital to know. Without the knowledge of these, together with regeneration, or the new birth, we hesitate not to say a man cannot be a Christian. Christ, who is admitted to be " *the Truth*," said so. " Except a man be born again, he cannot see the kingdom of God." The lineaments of all the great doctrines of God are plainly seen in the striking rituals of this place, and in the place itself.

Wonderful epitome of all the great things of God have we in this symbol. The day was an historic day for the whole race and for all time when Christ died ; and when God said in the garden, the seed of the woman shall bruise the serpent's head, it was a day to be remembered. The Tabernacle is the first full explanation of what He would be. Truly, He would be a suffering One.

It is an evil day this, in which but few seem alive to the awful fruit of these denials. " Take away the record of the Fall," said Archbishop Trench, " and of the present consequences of the Fall, and the provision God has made to repair those consequences, to build up the breach which Adam had made—take them away, and you take away the key of knowledge to all the rest of the Bible."

It is in the study of the Tabernacle pre-eminently the key is so plainly seen. It was not because of any delight in suffering that God instituted sacrifices, it arose out of an earnest, settled purpose; the suffering of death was the one great term in the eternal covenant which gave Christ His redeemed. The fire, long burning on the Altar, consuming to ashes their sacrifices, very plainly told this; it showed what God's estimate of sin was, and how death was the only way in which its doom could come. We may well therefore now turn our thoughts to

THE LORD'S OWN SUFFERINGS IN DEATH.

What we have insisted on are the facts, but we have not said historically what they were. And now for a little St. Mark is our guide; he says, on approaching Christ's sufferings, "They came to a place which was named Gethsemane," a plot of ground, it would seem, suited to the impending moment, for it was there the Man of sorrows oft-times resorted to pray. It was sweet to fortify Himself by communion with His Father in heaven.

Peter, James, and John were with Him when He began to be "sore amazed," and to be "very heavy," evidently utterly, helplessly exhausted. Deep horror seized Him, it was *the cross* that He had to reach, and this woe lay upon His soul. Martyrs had the former, they were sawn asunder, burnt alive, speared, tortured, tormented,

but their souls were free; they felt no sin, no
wrath, no sting of death. The garden was

THE APPROACH TO THE CROSS.

Falling to the ground, He prayed, "Abba,
Father"—that is, "Father, Father;" the one word
Hebrew, the other Greek—"all things are possible
unto Thee, take away this cup from Me." He
had said, "Lo, I come to do Thy will, O God."
Ere He could reach the place of doom, it would
seem as if His very strength to bear Him to the
cross might fail. Was this one of the occasions,
when He says, "Who in the days of His flesh,
when He had offered up prayers and supplications,
with strong crying and tears unto Him that was
able to save Him from death"? And was it in
reference to the same He Himself said, as if anticipating the agony in the garden, "He weakened
My strength in the way; He shortened My days.
I said, O My God, take Me not away in the midst
of My days"? But in the divine reply He
is not cut off. Magnificent words, as if God
had said, "Cut off"?—"*Thy years are throughout all generations.* Of old hast Thou laid the
foundation of the earth : and the heavens are the
work of Thy hands. They shall perish, but *Thou
shalt endure :* yea, all of them shall wax old like a
garment; as a vesture shalt Thou change them,
and they shall be changed : but *Thou art the same,*

and Thy years shall have no end." This as to His
Godhead. Then His reward : "The children of
Thy servants shall continue, and their seed shall
be established before Thee." What words! Oh,
blessed Lord, if we sorrow over Thy sorrows,
which we do, we joy over Thy glorious standing
as Son, as the Eternal One. He needed what
God had for Him—

THE HELPING ANGEL,

who strengthened Him ; but it was more than an
angel. It was God Himself assuring Him—yea,
assuring us — of who and what He was — the
God-man, the Christ of God, the Maker of the
world. It was in the midst of this scene that
Peter, James, and John had the opportunity of
watching with Him. Sadly they lost that opportunity. Gethsemane was never repeated. "Sleep
on now" was a touching word to them, as it has
been to thousands since, who during their one life
have lost all that that life could ever bestow.

And what sustained Him in Gethsemane was,
"*He is near that justifieth Me.*" Wonderful
word! If He had stood in His own Person
merely, and upon His own foundations, there
had been no occasion for such a declaration.
"Innumerable evils," He says, "have compassed
Me about." Oh, are we not overwhelmed with
looking at *one* solitary life of sin—a dark, dark

line of sin running all through, from childhood
to the grave? But He was "*made sin*," as if sin
itself; and sins—the sins of all His redeemed, with
all their vileness and blackness of evil—were as
if His own. Think of this, oh, my soul—three
hours of darkness! this was on the cross, not
in the garden; the darkness without, and the
darkness within. For what else could it be but
darkness where all was blackness and vileness of
guilt, shut up to deserved wrath? Satan too, His
great enemy, had full power for displaying His
enmity. It was his hour. But the suffering Son
of man, with no God to succour, alas! who can
tell what that was?

> "We may not know, we cannot tell,
> What pains He had to bear."

Daniel and Jeremiah, with others, in their woes
never cried, "Eloi, Eloi . . . My God, My God, why
hast Thou forsaken Me." Instead of wrath they
had God's comforting presence; yet His wrath
lay hard on His own Son, ah, yes! indeed, our
load of guilt was there. It was *judicial:* it was
God's mighty testimony against sin. Christ
justified God in bearing His justice; this He did
by word and act. And when He could do or say
no more, and had been hanging helpless on the
accursed tree, to which He had been affixed with
the awful nails driven by the hand of man, He

opened His heart and spake in blood—in *death*. Oh, my soul, what a history is this to know and to accept! It was God dealing with *our* sins.

And here let me say, it was not a work, as some suppose, to be ascribed to the mere natural cross. The literal instrument was merely a piece of wood, and, where it stood, only a few inches in diameter. But who was it hung on this cross? Into whose hands and feet were the nails driven? Whose head was pierced with the mock crown of thorns? On this one has well said—

> " Not to Thy cross, but to Thyself,
>   My living Saviour, would I cling ;
> 'Twas Thou, and not Thy cross, that bore
>   My soul's dark guilt—sin's deadly sting."

And what were the issues of it? Hanging on two nails, an awful cry—called by some " His orphan cry "—was heard, saying, " My God, My God, why hast Thou forsaken Me?" Godward, there was an infinite meaning in these words ; manward, they told that man in his sins was far from God, as the brink of hell from heaven. And yet this was because God would bring man nigh. Since Eden he had not seen the Face of God ; conscience told him he could not see Him as he was. The law was aggravating beyond all degree with its "thou *shalt*" and "thou shalt *not*" to one who could not and would not. The only answer he

could have given to these was, "Why to satisfy
the law I must not be a sinner at all." But what
did this death do? It showed the sinful could be
saved : Christ, as the Gift of God's love, and in
order to satisfy God and save man, had entered
the very dominion into which sin had brought
man, and where sin was reigning by *death*. He
died, He rose again. Conscience, and law, and
the reigning power—sin—are dismantled of their
claim, and man may now see the Face of God and
live. In proof God raised Him from the dead, what
else could give confidence that our sins have been
done away—what but the resurrection of our Lord
Jesus Christ? And what is His glorious resurrection
but the evidence that He could not be holden by
death? You must come to a right understanding
of that passage, He "was delivered for our offences,
and raised again for our justification." He was
delivered *because* we were sinners ; He was raised
again *because* we were righteous. It is because the
sins of God's people have been blotted out "as a
thick cloud" that the Lord Jesus Christ has been
raised from the dead, and now sits at the right
hand of God, the evidence to every believing soul
that he is justified. We cannot receive this too
simply. That the act of justification of all God's
people was perfected by the death of the Lord
Jesus would appear clearly set forth in such

passages as "justified by His blood," "He hath made Him to be sin for us, who knew no sin; that we might be made the righteousness of God in Him." His body was not to decay, death would never bring it to man's kindred dust. How it takes from the grave its damps, and from death its terrors, to think of Joseph's tomb, where we seem to hear the words, "Thou wilt shew Me the path of life." Very precious to think of this un-suffering and peaceful Form as it had been anointed with the sweet spices by him who once had come to Him by night. The shittim wood tells how the body may die, but not dissolve. His own forecasting of it was, "Thou wilt not leave My soul in hell, neither wilt Thou suffer Thine holy One to see corruption," hence His tomb was sweet and pure as heaven itself. Never man had lain there before.

> "Come, see the place! In lowly reverence bow,
> Nor stone nor seal forbids thine entrance now;
> Fear not to gaze within the silent tomb,
> A risen Lord has stolen away the gloom.
> The very grave henceforth is circled round
> With resurrection-glory newly found."

Angels found it

A PALACE OF DELIGHT.

I have often thought that they, and not He, had folded the napkin at the head; for He had done with it, and left, where His body had been, the linen clothes unfolded still ; suggestively, the members have not yet left their graves, or have not been called to Him their Head. Question: Would the angels have preferred remaining in their own heaven to this visit of theirs to the tomb of Joseph? I imagine not. And now, what of our own tomb? Precious words, "Because I live, ye shall live also;" if we die, our dust will rest in hope. Why need we fear?

> "The graves of all His saints He blest,
>   And softened every bed ;
>   Where should the dying members rest,
>   But with their living Head?"

And how calmly, all sorrows hushed, and sufferings over :

> "The storms that wreck this wintry sky,
>   No more disturb their sweet repose
>   Than summer evening's latest sigh
>   That shuts the rose."

Oh, glorious gospel! Oh, news most wonderful! Christ saves *sinners*. Are you saying, "I should like to be saved; I wish I were saved, but I am not; I would like to be in heaven; I would like to be a child of God; I would fain call Him Father, but it cannot be"? What is the answer to all this? The answer is, *Christ.* He was in death, because of sin, outside God's presence;

after that death we are as He is, freed from the death which He took; and as to God and heaven, what you want are title and fitness to be there. For this "Christ is made of God unto us wisdom, and righteousness, and sanctification, and redemption," all which you could not be yourself; so now, what barrier is there? None. Therefore this is

PERFECT PEACE.

This is the gospel. Come, always come without money; "yea, come, buy wine and milk without money and without price;" come, with nothing to bring excepting Christ; and the very first moment we see Christ thus, we are not any longer lost, or standing helpless before the bar of censure or the law, but saved. "Shall not perish;" [the word is, shall not be lost], "but have everlasting life." And now sweet is gratitude. "We love Him because He first loved us." "As the Father hath loved Me, so have I loved you."

"Lord, Thou hast loved me, and henceforth to me
    Earth's noonday is but gloom;
  My soul sails forth on the eternal sea,
    And leaves the shore of doom.

"I pass within the glory even now,
    Where shades and words are not;
  For joy that passeth words, O Lord, art Thou,
    A bliss that passeth thought.

"I enter there, for Thou hast borne away
    The burden of my sin;
  With conscience clear as heaven's unclouded day,
    Thy courts I enter in.

"Heaven now for me, for ever Christ and heaven—
    The endless NOW begun;
  No *promise*, but a gift eternal *given*,
    Because the work is done."

Precious, glorious is our sense of salvation, to know it, oh, how blessed! what can we render to the Lord? Oh, soul of mine, what canst thou do? what canst thou render? Service? Worship? Adoration? Praise? Blessed Lord! Such a Saviour! Such a salvation!

> "I cannot serve Thee as I ought,
>   No works have I to boast;
> But I shall glory in the thought,
>   That I shall owe Thee most."

Take one more look.

HIS WORK IS PERFECT

The "ashes" tell of this; grand, consoling is the truth taught by those ashes; the fire went up in righteousness, having done its work; but the ashes—self and sin—went downward out of view; as we and thousands more have sung—

> "With ashes who would grudge to part,
>   When called on angels' food to feast?"

"The pan" was for the ashes; downward into the net they descended. Hence they were taken to the place assigned them, so that as the hosts of the Lord moved on in the wilderness journey, living on angels' food, the manna from heaven, and drinking of the water from the "rock that followed them," these all were left behind. Blessed the sight to lose, and God's voice to hear, saying, "Your sins and your iniquities will I remember no more." But ere we close here, let us listen to a few of God's own witnesses. They form a lovely

PAGE OF TESTIMONY.

How these views were held by godly men in the past we may see from such as the

PIOUS GODWIN.

He asks, "What need was there for any justi-fication of Christ, if He had not been in some way near a condemnation? He therefore must be supposed to stand at God's tribunal, as well as at Pilate's, with all our sins upon Him; and so the prophet tells us God made the iniquity of us all to meet on Him. He was made a curse, and stood not in danger of Pilate's condemnation only, but of God's, unless He satisfied Him for all those sins; and when the wrath of God for sin came thus upon Him, His faith was put to it, to wait and trust in God for justification, to take off all those sins together with His wrath from Him, and to acknowledge Himself satisfied and then acquitted. The twenty-second psalm, made for Christ when hanging on the tree, speaks of how His heart was taken up; that while He is brought in, as putting forth such as here we speak of when He called God His God, we find Him in that psalm laying Himself at God's feet, lower than any man ever did. 'I am a worm,' He said, 'that every man treads on, and counts it a matter of nothing to kill,' and ' no man.' All this because He bore our sins. *The business with which He trusted God was, that He should rise again, and be acquitted from them.* Neither did He exercise faith for Himself only, but for us also. This is a great truth, considering the infinite number of the saved. God trusted Christ before He came into the world, and saved many of the Jews upon His bare word; and then at His death Christ trusted God again, for the Jews and Gentiles; yea, and all that were to believe after His death. And here let us note especially how this example of Christ may teach and incite us to believe. Hast thou, my soul, the guilt of innumerable transgressions coming in and discouraging thee from trusting to Him? Consider what Christ had, though not His own."

It may be bold, but true is the utterance of

LUTHER:

"Christ was dealt with as the greatest sinner that ever was—that is, by imputation for the sins of God's chosen met on Him—yet He trusted in God to be justified from them all, and to be raised up from the wrath due to them. Yet art thou but one poor sinner, and thy faith hath but a light and small load laid upon it—namely, thine own sins—which to the sum He undertook for us are but a unit few compared to an infinite number."

A SPANISH MARTYR

writes: "When I speak of faith, I mean that which lives in the soul, not attained by human exertion and tact, but by means of the grace of God by supernatural light, a faith which embraces all God's word, His threats no less than His promises, so that he, when he hears that Christ said, 'He who believes shall be saved,' his faith in these words, which he fully holds, inspires such confidence that he has not the slightest doubt about his salvation."

LADY POWERSCOURT,

alluding to her own sorrows, and comparing them with those of Christ's death—sorrows, when He

had no such sympathy as was given to her,
writes :

> " Jesus, my sorrow lies too deep
>   For human sympathy ;
>   It knows not how to tell itself
>   To any but to Thee.

> " Yes ; for as if Thou wouldst be God,
>   E'en in Thy misery,
>   There's been no sorrow but Thine own
>   Untouched by sympathy.

> " Jesus, my fainting spirit brings
>   Its fearfulness to Thee ;
>   Thine eye, at least, can penetrate
>   The clouded mystery."

EBENEZER ERSKINE

" I know that when my soul forsakes this
tabernacle of clay, it will fly as naturally to my
Saviour's bosom as the bird to its beloved nest."

DR. DODDRIDGE

" I have no hope in what I have been or
done. In Him I trust; in Him I have strong
consolation, and shall assuredly be accepted in
this Beloved of my soul."

DR. M'CALL

" I am a great sinner; I have been a great
sinner ; but my trust is in Jesus Christ, and what
He has done and suffered for sinners."

ROBERT HALDANE

"I have no righteousness of my own. There is no merit in any of my works; but my trust has been and is, that Christ is my righteousness."

CHARLES WESLEY

" Just and holy is Thy name,
   I am all unrighteousness ;
   Vile and full of sin I am,
   Thou art full of truth and grace."

TOPLADY

" Nothing in my hand I bring,
   Simply to Thy cross I cling ;
   Naked, come to Thee for dress ;
   Helpless, look to Thee for grace ;
   Vile, I to the fountain fly ;
   Wash me, Saviour, or I die !"

Precious testimonies, showing how sin and Christ's death for sin, and righteousness reckoned to the sinner that believes, have been seen as eternal verities by thousands of the students of God's word.

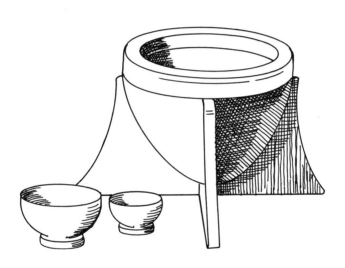

The Brazen Laver

5

The Laver

"Ye are washed, ye are justified."—1 Corinthians 6:11

JUSTIFICATION is a complete clearance out of God's judicial court; but that does not say that we are fit for the Divine presence in full enjoyment of it; therefore, we are to be perfectly clean—sanctified. All the offerings were this; they were put into the Laver and so made clean, and were then placed upon the altar; *i.e.*, all the sweet savour offerings which represented the perfectness of Christ.

We tread a defiling world, and from the defilement of our practical walk in it, we need to be cleansed: God holds this to be of great moment. Twice it is shown that if Aaron entered without resorting to the Laver, he must die; this was sufficiently solemn. The washing is not for salvation, but for purification. Besides what it is for me before God, it is of vast practical moment as to myself. Supposing I want communion, and the enjoyment of service for God, I cannot have these unless living in the spirit of the Laver; if I have sin on my conscience, and do not know this Laver practically, I cannot enjoy God. I may essay to go into His presence for communion, but with what result; it is myself and my conscience that exercise the mind instead of the enjoyment of God.

Here confession is what is needed, followed by the promised forgiveness; and He who tells you to confess *will* forgive; He is faithful and just to do this; faithful to Christ who bore the sin; faithful to Himself and to you. Every moment you delay is a moment of unbelief, sin allowed is like a disease neglected; but touch this Laver, that is Christ, anew, and you will be healed. There is not only life, but restoration in a look at the crucified One. God's requirement is absolute purity, this we have only in Christ; any progress of ours must ever be a matter of degree only, and therefore could never reach that requirement.

This sets aside all purification of self as a ground of our standing before God, and shows what good news the gospel brings when it tells us we are complete in Him, that God, through Christ, has made us clean every whit, so that we are as Christ is before God.

Some, indeed, vainly say they have no sin. Do they know what sin is, or will they deny this Laver, or Christ's office as Priest? Aaron, contracting the desert sand in his foot, or the assoilment of his hands, told of the defiling influences of the way. The Laver met this need. As the scene of it was between the priest coming in, and where God was in His sanctuary, so Christ, now in heaven, who is our Laver, is between our daily life and God. As no stain on Aaron could go beyond the Laver, so no sin of ours can go beyond Christ.*
The Laver, moreover, was in the presence of the altar, where sin had been judged and put away. Could a believer's sin reach heaven, Christ's hands and feet and side would be witness against it, saying it could have no place there.

What rest is this to the heart that knows it! Sweet in this light is the word, "Come unto Me, all ye that labour and are heavy laden, and I will give you rest." Yes, both for atonement and daily sin, He is our never-changing rest before God, to whom, as washed and clean every whit, He delights to bring us, and in whom we are as He is righteous, holy, "accepted in the Beloved." This blessedly is our history.

The priests were not to wash *in* the Laver, but *in the water drawn from it.* The base or

* See this more fully in "Hosea."

foot was probably detached from the basin, we read, his foot was also of brass, indicating that, though it was one Laver, it was in two distinct parts. The upper part was filled with water from the streams which flowed from the stricken rock; this was always ready with its supply for the lower part, from which it was drawn for use. Only in the foot did they wash. Both parts represent Christ, as we have been reminded—Christ in heaven the true water of life, and Christ giving His supplies according to our need here on earth; keeping us in a wilderness world, when all around and within subject us to their defiling influences.

What we want is to walk even as Christ walked. "Every man that hath this hope in Him purifieth himself, even as He is pure." The nearer we get to realize this hope the further we shall want to get from self and from sinful ways of the heart and life. Christ is our blessed model; " He that saith he abideth in Him ought himself also so to walk, even as He walked:" we know how holily He walked, how forgivingly, how separately from sinners. Line upon line have we on this remarkable type. In 1 Kings vii. 23 we have it described as a molten sea, having its place, not in the desert, but in the Temple—an enlargement of the one in the Tabernacle. It stood upon twelve oxen, three looking north, three looking south, three looking east, and three west; the brim was wrought with flowers and lilies, and it contained two thousand baths. In verses 26–30 we see that, whilst the Laver itself could hold two thousand baths, at the basis was the provision for washing the hands and feet. Why, compared with the Tabernacle, was there this difference? I believe it shows that in the day of the earth's glory the value and efficacy of the sanctifying power of the death of Christ will have a tenfold manifestation. In that day God promises to bring His people back into their land, to give them a new heart, and take away the stony hearts out of their flesh; and He says, "I will sprinkle clean water upon you, and ye shall be clean." This refers to the millennial time, showing how Christ will not only have taken away all sin, but that the people will be all righteous.

Beautiful is the description of the brim of the Laver. The best of nature was there—flowers intertwined around and noble animals supporting it. It is Eden again, its beauties more than restored. The groan of creation in that day has ceased. In the heavenly state, when it will be ours to be with the Lord, it will not be a sea of water for washing, but a sea of glass, manifesting holiness permanent—for ever the same.

Let us specially note that when Israel journeyed there was no covering for the Laver as there was for others of the types. Whether this was to teach it as always available is not said; but this we know, there never can come a moment for us that there is not God's provision at hand—Christ our High Priest, with the value of His whole work, appearing in the presence of God for us.

The Laver was not merely for purity, but for refreshment. How refreshed would Aaron enter into the sanctuary after the Laver. How refreshed did the Lord desire His disciples to be ere they sat down with Him at that last paschal supper, and the supper in His own precious remembrance, which He then instituted for the first time. Therefore by some a close connection has been supposed between that remarkable pitcher of water the disciples were to discover and the guest-chamber where He was to have the paschal feast. At all events, John xiii. shows He did then and there wash their weary, wayworn feet. Can they ever forget it, and the meaning of it all? Whom He loved, He loved to the end.

Oh, my soul, why not, with such provision, be always free, always happy, always ready for realized communion with God?

6

The Holy Place

"By His own blood He entered in once into the holy place, having obtained eternal redemption for us."—Hebrews 9:12

THE name here is significant—"Holy Place." How clearly this manifests what God Himself is in divine perfection; He is absolutely holy. His house must be holy; He enjoins it upon us, "Be ye holy; for I am holy." He is called by the name "Holy" and the "Holiest." I like what is recorded as the saying of a good man, how that "every declaration of what God is in His character is a rebuke to us; that it expresses to us our own ugliness; for if we were as we ought to be, God would only have to say, 'I am God'—that would be enough. When He says, 'I am a holy God,' or 'I am a God of truth,' or 'I am righteous,' it is as much as to say we are so dull of understanding, so slow to learn, that He is obliged, as it were, to distribute Himself into parts, according to our necessities. Hence He is pleased at one time to

hold up one perfection of His character for our
contemplation.   At another time He places before
us another grand feature."

But now respecting the Holy Place itself; many
things come to mind as we enter, and, first of all,
Christ risen from the dead.   How soft its silence,
so different from the scene of agony and death
of the sin-offering outside the camp, or the slaying
and dying of the offerings for the brazen altar!
The one is Christ crucified, the other is Christ
a risen and glorified Man in heaven.

THE SYMBOLS

are beautiful.   We see altars of pure gold sur-
mounted with crowns of gold, bread of the finest
flour, and incense of purest odour; curtains too of
many colours, laden with cherubim beautifully
woven therein.   Besides these, Aaron in his holy
garments for beauty and for glory (or "honour,"
as the word is), typifying the great truth of
Christ in divine acceptance for us, seated at the
right hand of God crowned with glory and honour.
Splendid emblem of this is Aaron, his offices, the
gold and incense, the crowns, the brilliants on
the breast, and all his garments.   The scene is
wonderful, affording a sweet change from the
tumultuous cries of the dying sacrifices we saw
outside, for here every object is a symbol of some

calm glory of Christ; I repeat it, not Christ in
death, but risen from the dead, and ascended into
heaven.

What we have seen was rather the historical
fact of Christ having risen, of which the evidences
are infallible. If the four evangelists had been
four deceivers, they would all have written much
the same thing; but, like a lovely landscape, one
part of which differs from all the rest, yet the
whole forming a complete picture, so with these
four accounts.

Sweeter than the dawn of creation was the dawn
of that morning when He rose from the dead;
more glorious His own one word, saying, "All
hail," than all the voices combined of the sons of
God, who shouted together for joy on seeing sun,
moon, and stars, and this planetary orb, all taking
their position in the vast field of His creative
power. What a twilight! What a sweet hush of
surprise when the Mary-mother and the Magdalene-
Mary saw the stone which was between them and
their beloved Dead rolled aside, and the mouth
of the tomb left wide open. Inside, angels sitting,
as if at perfect ease and delight, where death and
the tomb had been vanquished; outside, heaven
had taken possession of the stone — a bright,
glorious angel, sat upon it. Neither earth nor hell
dare dispute the possession. Added to this attitude

were the wondrous words, "ye seek Jesus, which
was crucified. He is not here: for He is risen, as
He said; go quickly, and tell His disciples that
He is risen." Nothing unwilling the two then
started with their heavenly message, when, lo, He
Himself stood before them, and said, "All hail."
What a morning! Principalities and powers, thrones
and dominions, all jubilant with the song, unlike
that at creation, which soon became marred by
the entrance of evil; but here the concentration
and the consummation of all Herod's evil design
was trodden down by the feet of Him who
ere yesterday was laid a corpse in that tomb
which had never seen corruption. As the gold
and silver vessels of the sanctuary were hung
up on their appointed nail, so our hope of immortality, and of all the glories involved therein,
are now hung on this Master of assemblies, who
died but lives, and lives to die no more.

Thus what an expanse of interest! infinite
magnitude! sweet is it to linger here. Grandly
has He passed into the heavens which He has
newly furnished—furnished as never before with
Himself the God-man. None of the angels had
ever seen a God-man in heaven. It is Christ
in human nature, at the right hand of the Majesty
on high, crowned with glory and honour; strong
foundation! Paul said, "if Christ be not risen,

then is our preaching vain, and your faith is also vain . . . ye are yet in your sins." Hence at this foundation of our faith, unbelief deals its blows, but how vainly. Besides the circumstances of Christ's resurrection, five hundred eye-witnesses at once are too much for them.

CHRIST RISEN IS OUR STRONG FOUNDATION

A story is told of Lepaux, a member of the French Directory, that with much thought and study he had invented a new religion to be called "Theophilanthropy," a kind of organised Rousseauism, and that, being disappointed in its not being readily approved and adopted, he complained to Talleyrand of the difficulty he found in introducing it.

"I am not surprised," said Talleyrand, "at the difficulty you find in your effort. It is no easy matter to introduce a new religion. But there is one thing I would advise you to do, and then, perhaps, you might succeed."

"What is it? what is it?" asked the other with eagerness.

"It is this," said Talleyrand: "Go and be crucified, and then be buried, and then rise again on the third day, and then go on working miracles, raising the dead, and healing all manner of diseases, and casting out devils, and then it is possible that you might accomplish your end !"

And the philosopher, crest-fallen and confounded, went away silent.

The anecdote shows, in a fresh and striking light, how firm the foundation on which Christianity and the faith of the Christian rest. "Ransack all history," says an able writer, "and you cannot find a single event more satisfactorily proved than the resurrection of Christ from the dead." And says another, a distinguished jurist : "If human evidence has ever proved, or ever can prove anything, then the miracles of Christ are proved beyond a shadow of a doubt." And yet the miracles and resurrection of Christ prove His divinity; and as Napoleon said, "His divinity once admitted, Christianity appears with the precision and clearness of algebra—it has the connection and unity of a science."

What a change for Christ Himself! rejected, cast out, slain by man, greeted by God, worshipped by angels, having with Him His many sons in the glory, He our own Forerunner. Conceive of this Christ of God having had God's wrath lying hard on Him for our sins, and God even forsaking Him, having now put away sin. The words in the gospel and Psalm xxii. 31 are the same. In one it is said "*finished ;*" in the other "*done:*" both signifying that His work was accomplished.

But now He is in heaven to die no more, with all the fulness of the Godhead bodily in Him; so that He is God, and He is there occupied about us; what more could we possibly want? Wonderful work! wonderful change! What welcomes! what floods of glory ready to flow in upon Him! Heaven itself is a great change. And suggestively here we may be reminded of how it will be with us in our far less degree, when, having closed our eyes upon all that was sin and sorrow here, our heavenly home opens to our view. The bird at night folds its head under its wing for the time of sleep, only to lift it anew at dawn, amidst the light and joy of returning day; the image of that "wide ethereal, when the invisible will crowd" upon the departed one, who, "absent from the body," is "present with the Lord." For us what a contrast—this bodily frame dissolved, or, if we die not, changed, and we emerge at once, in the twinkling of an eye, into the blessedness of His revealed presence! How precious

THE UNFOLDING OF SCRIPTURE

on such a Christ, and on this our own blessedness! What other book could tell such secrets concerning eternity? it is solitary and alone in its supremacy; poor and wretched are all surmises of man, left to his own unassisted reason. How beautiful our imaginings when guided by Scripture! the life under the feathers of the Almighty—in death; no change as to that. Could any other book give rise to so sweet a hymn of the dead as the one sung by the early Church over their beloved departed ones ?

> " Sleep on, beloved, sleep and take thy rest,
>> Lay down thy head upon thy Saviour's breast ;
>> We love thee well, but Jesus loves thee best—
>>> Good-night.

> " Calm is thy slumber as an infant's sleep,
>> But thou shalt wake no more to toil and weep :
>> Thine is a perfect rest, secure and deep—
>>> Good-night.

> " Until the shadow from this earth be cast,
>> Until He gather in His sheaves at last,
>> Until the twilight gloom be overpast—
>>> Good-night.

> " Until the Easter glory light the skies,
>> Until the dead in Jesus shall arise,
>> And He shall come, but not in lowly guise—
>>> Good-night.

> " Until made beautiful by love divine,
>> Thou in the likeness of thy Lord shalt shine,
>> And He shall bring that golden crown of thine—
>>> Good-night.

> " Only ' good-night,' beloved, not ' farewell ! '
>> A little while, and all His saints shall dwell
>> In hallowed union, indivisible—
>>> Good-night.

" Until we meet again before His throne,
    Clothed in the spotless robe He gives His own,
    Until we know even as we are known—
                    Good-night." *

What other book than our own Holy Bible ever led to praises, or pretended to comfort at the grave ? The poet speaks of

" The dear churchyard's sod ;"

and dear it is, attended with happy memories of those we loved, and the consolations of divine hope. It has been sweet there to hear the voice of Jesus : " I am the resurrection and the life," and " thy brother shall rise again ;" and to the heart of the mother bereaved of her child, " I shall go to him, but he shall not return to me." How to contemplate our own removal and change into this glory, 2 Corinthians iv. 5 is our guide. As one has written :

" They err who tell us that the spirit, unclothed,
    And from its mortal tabernacle loosed,
    Has neither lineament of countenance,
    Nor limit of ethereal mould, nor form
    Of spiritual substance."†

But the great thing with a Christian is how to live; living brightly here, and then a bright removal.

---

* The early Christians were accustomed to bid their dying friends " Good-night," so sure were they of their awakening on the resurrection morning.

† BICKERSTETH.

Grand is the sun as to his going down ; who has
not been arrested with the beauteous glory of the
setting luminary, descending full-orbed, with its
well-known golden splendour, leaving behind a
long line of glorious rays to tell that he has been,
and still is, lighting up the place of his departure.
Sometimes it is more like a molten sea, reminding
one of what the golden scenes of heaven must be.
I have thought of Dr. Watts's lovely hymn on the
sweet analogy between the departing orb and the
dying child of God.   The sun not lost when gone
from view, but shining in another hemisphere—the
Christian when he dies, but gone to a brighter and
happier world.   The sun leaving behind him rays
of glory, which linger long ; the Christian, full of
faith and love, leaving the precious memory of
what he was long after his peaceful exit to be with
the Lord.   I have known such, nearing ninety
years, like the sun, full-orbed, and more and more
beauteous at his going down ; the aged fingers on
the instrument, and the voice accompanying it
with—

> " How sweet the name of Jesus sounds
>   In a believer's ear."

And as I gazed upon his aged form, I marvelled
at the unction and power and sweetness of a soul
so bordering on the eternal world.   " The path of
the just is as the shining light which shineth more

and more until the perfect day." As the night
accumulates rapidly, we are like Paul's company
when "they wished for the day," as if their very
longing for the day brought them some relief.
The darkest hour is before the dawn ; these are
last times. There are trials, difficulties, long sick-
nesses, placing down beneath the sod of the valley
those who journeyed together in times past. The
Divine nature gives us to be more akin to that
blessed country, longing for the pinions of a
dove. If there is anything you have not yet
got from the Lord, get it instantly, so that you
may say, " Oh that I had wings !" " I would not
live alway." The Lord has said, " I go away,
and will come again for you." This is true and
glorious. We shall be "caught up" in the clouds
to meet *Him ;* that is a day which will dawn
and never have a cloud, never have an end.
Through eighteen hundred years that word still
sounds—" I will come again;" " Be of good cheer."
Darkness is passing, joy is nearing. Our joy
should increase in proportion as the Day is approaching. The nearer to our last breath, the
more brilliant, the more peaceful we should be.
As earth takes up the light of heaven and reflects
it, so as we get near God we get fortitude, and our
end is *peace.*

Finally, all got "safe to land," and so will it

be with us. The whole Church of God, wherever they may be, glory awaits us. May my God awaken the desire in every heart!

> " It is not weariness of life
>   That makes us wish to die,
>   But we are drawn by cords which come
>   From out Eternity."

Truly Scripture is precious. Luther has said: " Holy Scripture is a sweet-scented herb," and that the more you rub it, the more it emits its fragrance. And Tholuck on this says: " Never certainly have I rubbed it enough. I cleave so much to the ingenious thoughts of men and the things of the learned. And yet the Bible is a deep ocean; whereas learned men, even when their cogitations are shrewdest, are water cisterns, and in seasons of need sometimes run dry and sometimes congeal." In approaching the Word of God I must empty myself of my own thoughts; when our hands are full we can receive no more. We have need to plead—

> " Oh, search my inmost thoughts, that they
>   May never from Thy precepts stray!
>   Guide heart and mind
>   Thy truth to find."

But the blessed Bible, like this Tabernacle, is superhuman. And here I would like to add another word—the subject so important in this day. "The difference between it and all other books," remarks another, "is not a difference of degree—that one is a little more inspired than another. No; the one is human, the other is superhuman; the one is discoursed, the other is delivered; the one is the working of man's mind, the other is the supernatural communication of a supernatural salvation for man. The four points often on my mind are supremacy, sufficiency, intelligence, and infallibility." We could not do without infallibility; living or dying we need the certainty that led Paul to say, "I know whom I have believed." And we need certainty for those we love. Can any one not be moved by the thought of what they will lose, who having neglected Christ will be certain only of eternal separation? what misery! what endless regrets! What a hell in hell, the remembrance of the summer of life ended in vain, and the harvest of opportunity lost for ever! oh, pangs of remorse, how dreadful for ever! To the child of God, how blessed are the certainties of this Holy Place! what wondrous calm! what peace! The gold, the bread, and all else seen in softest radiance from the lamp. Happy, O my soul, to be on this side the veil where Jesus is, and where all these happy associations come to mind. Christ risen from the dead, and sin for ever put away;

God satisfied; a banquet spread. Light divine surrounding each object from the light-stands of pure massive gold. What numberless lines of thought have we here! Truths infinite!

Beautiful the omissions. First of all there is

NO LIGHT FROM WITHOUT,

and there shall be night no more. "They need no light of the sun: for the Lord God giveth them light." No light from without is here; no window, no aperture, through which any external ray of sun or moon could enter. And then, secondly, there is

NO GOLDEN PAVEMENT

or street of gold on which to tread. It is the bare earth—the ground common to the wilderness. Though by faith we are surrounded by glories which tell of Christ and heaven, we are yet children of the desert. "Thou turnest man to destruction" reads (R.V.) "Thou turnest man to *dust*." This is suggestive to us. It was from the dust we were taken, and, till the Lord come, to dust we return; and if the Lord tarry the grave is our house. Satan, our great adversary, comes to mind here; when this age has been rescued from his long grasp, in his overthrow and deep humiliation he will be made to eat the dust, reminding him of that day when as serpent, he made man to fall. But though only dust, the Tabernacle was on an even place; it is all even where God is; and in communion with Him we have no need to say, "My feet were almost gone, my steps had well-nigh slipped." It was when void of such communion David fell and Peter made denial of his Lord. Who that knows the sinfulness of the heart and the weakness of the flesh but must pray, "Hold Thou me up, and I shall be safe." There were, thirdly,

NO SORROWS.

If some priest or Levite, or any nearest and dearest to Aaron died, he could wear no mourning. The least sign of death has no place in heaven. "Sorrow and sighing" as if conscious of their unfitness "flee away." Sweet thus to think how it will be when we see as we are seen, and know as we are known. Aaron at times may have heard a sound of the camp outside. Possibly in heaven we may have some intimations of those yet journeying, with whom we have often together sung—

> "Loved ones are gone before,
>   Whose pilgrim days are done ;
> I soon shall meet them on that shore
>   Where partings are unknown."

And now I must speak of the symbols, for all this by the way. There yet remains specially to be noted the holy and beauteous furniture of the place, and most prominently first

THE GOLDEN LIGHT-STAND,

remarkable for its pure gold and its sevenfold lights; it consists of a base and stock with seven branches, three on each side and one in the middle. The branches are ornamented with flowers of lilies and pomegranates seventy in number. On the extremities of the branches, richly laden with ornaments, are the lamps.

Josephus remarks of it thus: "The first part, the Holy Place, contained three admirable pieces of workmanship, most admirable, and universally celebrated—a candlestick, a table, and an altar of incense, on which were fragrant spices, with which it was replenished from the sea, and from all lands inhabited and uninhabited." This he speaks concerning the Holy Place in the Temple. One more intelligent, of the vessel writes: "The one lamp-stand of gold in the Tabernacle was the type of ministry on earth in the power of the Spirit of God, having Christ for its centre, source, and subject. The ten golden lampstands in the Temple furnish us with another emblem of divine illumination in the power of that eternal Spirit who

The Golden Candlestick With Its Lamps and Vessels
(Uncovered and also partly covered)

searcheth all things, yea, the deep things of God. The risen saints will not only be radiant without with divine glory—the gold—and resplendent with every grace of the Spirit—the precious stones— but filled with divine light and revelation and knowledge within, as typified by these ten golden lampstands, with their seventy burning radiant lamps. In Rev. iv. 5 we read, 'And there were seven lamps of fire burning before the throne, which are the seven spirits of God.' This explains the emblem. The Spirit of God in the midst of the risen saints in heavenly glory will fill them with the perfection and completeness of spiritual wisdom and knowledge, of which seven lamps are the emblem. This wisdom and knowledge will not be cold and uninfluential, but warm, animating, and pure—seven lamps of fire burning." *

What a blaze of light the Spirit throws over the whole character and perfections of God, and over the whole question of sin; and over man, who would be an enigma indeed but for our divine knowledge. Christ is the wisdom of God—that wisdom by means of which we freely know all things, and without which man is not only in darkness, but in himself is darkness; as Paul said, "We who sometimes were darkness."

"The ten lampstands in the temple, five on each

* TRAIL'S translation.

side, seventy lamps in all, set forth spiritual knowledge in all its variety, fulness, and comprehensive-
ness. The ten golden lampstands were for the
sanctuary. The silver lampstands were probably
for use in the side chambers of the temple. The
golden lampstands of the sanctuary set forth divine
and spiritual truth realized in the presence of God.
The silver lampstands express spiritual truth held
in the communion of saints. Transcendantly
glorious indeed must the Holy Place have appeared, with its golden floor, its carved walls overlaid with purest gold, and glittering with precious
gems, its vaulted roof, and furnished with its altar
of incense, its tables of gold, and the whole filled
with the dazzling splendour of its many-shining
lamps." *

Particular notice is given respecting lighting and
trimming these lamps; when between the two
evens Aaron lighteth the lamps, he shall burn
incense upon it, a perpetual incense before the
Lord—a perpetual memorial of the preciousness
to God of His own beloved Son, and His
delight in His glorious finished work. We should
mingle a sense of the love of Christ, of His
preciousness to us, with all our light-shining
testimony.

Special command was given also respecting the

* *Englishman's Bible.*

oil for the light. The oil was from the olive tree; of this tree the cherubim in the Temple were made. This may suggest, at least, as to who they were not: angels would not be made out of that which represents the anointing of the Holy Ghost. The oil was to cause the lamps to burn continually; not, I imagine, that they were to burn without ceasing, for Aaron was to go in and light them from the evening to the morning, to show how all the light depended on the oil, just as all true wisdom, or ministry, or testimony depends on the Spirit.

The position of the lampstand was not in the Most Holy, but in the Holy Place; suggestively, we enjoy God here, ere we reach our heavenly home. We have now the Holy Ghost dwelling in us. We are now united to Christ just as the lamps were united to the golden shaft on which they were suspended; the lamps were dependent on the shaft just as the Church is dependent on Christ—safe, secure as Christ Himself. He says, "*Because* I live, ye shall live also." The lamps shed their light upon the shewbread, and upon the incense, and all else in this Holy Place—in other words, *upon Christ*. It is thus every Christian should direct his testimony to Christ; wherever his lot is cast, he should shine for Him as a light in the world; like John, we should say, "Behold the Lamb of God." The world is dark; and the Church alone through the Word can shine and reveal Christ; all else is dark.

It has been observed, respecting the trimming of the lamps, that we might think God would have said, "Take the lamps outside, and trim them there." But no, they were to be trimmed in the Holy Place; our lamps must be trimmed inside. That was where the prodigal was restored, not far off, but in his father's arms; not out in the world, but on the father's heart.

In keeping with this another has said, "These lamps were to be trimmed in the Holy Place, right under the eye of God; untrimmed lamps would smoke and smell. How often has sin spoilt our testimony, and sent forth an offensive smell instead of a sweet savour of Christ! The hidden or indulged sin of our hearts is the charred wick. We cannot remove this ourselves, we must take it into the Lord's presence, and sit down there; we must give Him time to talk to us, and show us our wrong thoughts, and correct our wrong judgments, and teach us His ways and His thoughts. Cleansing by *blood* is instantaneous, but cleansing or snuffing by *the Word* takes time; and this double cleansing is necessary in order to ensure victory over sin; He longs to see us shine brightly."

Note, but for the sevenfold lamps, all that was glorious within and around could never have been seen. Reminding us of Paul's words: "Eye hath not seen, nor ear heard, neither have entered into the heart of man, the things which God hath prepared for them that love Him, but God hath revealed them unto us by His Spirit: for the Spirit searcheth all things, yea, the deep things of God." These things are an outlook into the deep things of God, which we who believe now see. As the Holy Place would have been dark without the divine light, so man, however gifted and taught in his own reason, is utterly dark. Romans i. shows man had the knowledge of God; that he did not like to retain it; that he chose, instead of God, four-footed beasts and creeping things to worship, therefore God gave him up (the whole race, as I understand) to a reprobate mind, a mind void of judgment; so that man now under this judicial blindness cannot form a true knowledge for himself. Therefore a new start, a new beginning is needed; as the Lord said to Nicodemus, "Ye must be born again."

As in the old creation God had to say, "Let there be light," so with the new, by the mighty power of His Spirit in the awakening of a dead soul. The soul is all darkness till He in His gospel comes and gives light; He gives it only to faith. Hence one man's mind may be all intelligent on divine things, and another utterly ignorant; take, for example, Paul the apostle, while merely sitting at the feet of Gamaliel, with all the advantages of human learning—philosophy, science, religion—he was blind as to divine truth. But a child born of the Spirit of God would know the greatest of all knowledge when it could say, " I know whom I have believed;" and, " This is life eternal, that they might know Thee the only true God, and Jesus Christ, whom Thou hast sent." Alas! how little we see and use the light! Will the remembrance of it follow us? Shall we never call it to mind? Conceive that we have gone from this sublime scene, that at once we become absorbed in the enjoyment of Christ and of God. Ah, then! what then? may we not imagine the thought escaping us, What lives we have lived! How soon was our time spent! What if at such a moment the Lord were to say, " I know your thoughts; go back again to earth; live your little time again; live only for Me"? Coming back again to this world, could we live as we now do? Poor sorry Christians, poor unbelieving believers, are we at best. How befitting still the word, " Awake thou that sleepest, and arise from [among] the dead [the dead around], and Christ shall give

thee light !"   Many, alas ! have lamps, but no oil,
no new nature, no Spirit of God dwelling in them :
They are not born from above.   Remember the
five foolish virgins.   " I never knew you ;" words
never addressed to any inside the heavenly gate,
but to those who had profession, who had religion,
but no Christ.

Situated just inside the Tabernacle, over against
the candlestick, was

THE TABLE OF SHEWBREAD.

The " bread of the faces, or of the presence,"
says Saurin, "because constantly placed in God's
presence."   Malachi i. 7 calls it " *the table of the
Lord*," and the bread " *His meat.*"   God's affection
feeds on His Son, but the great thought here is
the provision there is for us in heaven lodged in
His Son.

In Leviticus xxiv. 6 it is called "the pure table."
It was a gold table.   It is "the bread of the
presence " (R.V.), as if to say this bread is suited
to be in the presence of God ; signifying not
merely " the bread of the presence," but the
" presence bread ;" for the table represents Christ,
the full amplification of which we see in His
wonderful discourse on the bread in John vi., "the
bread which came down from heaven."   The scene
here is in the Holy Place ; it is Aaron's work to

present it to God, as though he said: God has
many delights; but this is His chief delight, the
food on which He feasts: He has infinite affections,
and here is an object on which they may feed.
The Son of God from all eternity, from what He
is and has done, has ever feasted the love of God.
The bread was not only thus presented to God,
but Israel also had the value of the presentation.
When the high priest came in to put on his
garments for glory and for beauty, he had on his
breastplate the names of the twelve tribes; on
the table there was a loaf for each name. The
loaves were crowned with frankincense; the stones,
on which the names were engraved, were joined
by golden clasps to Aaron's breast, and as Aaron
bowed over the loaves, there was a loaf for each
stone, and though Naphtali was only one-tenth
the size of some of the other tribes, still the
loaves were the same. Suggestively, Paul will
not have a greater Christ than the malefactor
converted on the cross.

It was as though Israel presented the bread for
itself, and we ourselves are privileged to present
Christ to God. If our sins trouble us, we present
Him as the brazen altar; if troubled about our
walk, if there has been the sin and sorrow of a
downfall, we present Him as the officiating Priest
for us at the golden altar; if at the end of a life-

The Table of Shewbread

The Table of Shewbread Partly Covered

time of failure, and marked by sin all the way, still
Christ. The loaves were changed continually.
" There was never such a thing," says Dr. A. Bonar,
"as a mouldy loaf on that table." Aaron and his
sons never lived on a loaf that had lost its fresh-
ness ; and the Christian can never live on his past
experiences ; Christ should be more fresh to him
every day, the nearer heaven the more precious
Christ. Then notice the quantity of bread in each
loaf—two omers, twice too much for any one
person. The bread was always there ; Christ never
leaves us : we can never exhaust Christ ; though
all redeemed sinners live on Him, yet is He not
impoverished. Aaron and his sons had to appropriate the bread, Aaron was to go in on the
Sabbath morning, take it, break it up, and distribute it : it was life to those who received it,
reminding us of the Lord's discourse on the bread.
" Whoso eateth My flesh, and drinketh My blood,
hath eternal life ; and I will raise him up at the
last day." (John vi. 54.) Four times is it repeated,
" I will raise him up at the last day." If we have
only tasted a crumb of this bread, I can tell you
what will be our future ; for this is a promise
special and absolute, " I will raise him up at the
last day." This is not a general resurrection as
men speak of it, but a resurrection from among
the dead. " The Lord cometh," said Enoch, " with

ten thousand of His saints," which shows that they had been raised before, or they could not so come with Him. In the Temple there was an important difference regarding the table of shewbread; instead of one table there were ten, a tenfold display and a tenfold appropriation of Christ in the day of the coming glory. The Lord said, " Blessed are they which do hunger and thirst after righteousness ; for they shall be filled." Yes, "shall be filled." Happy certainty! They hunger; they are filled ; I do not believe in that kind of state which year after year says, "I *am* hungry; I *want* Christ." Did you ever see a man really hungry who did not at once grasp the bread when offered to him? Why thus so long in want when it is said, " He that cometh to Me shall never hunger; and he that believeth on Me shall never thirst"?

But now see another object of beauty and glory.

THE GOLDEN ALTAR ;

or, the altar of incense. This also is in the Holy Place. "And thou shalt make an altar to burn incense upon : of acacia wood (R.V.) shalt thou make it. A cubit shall be the length thereof, and a cubit the breadth thereof; foursquare shall it be : and two cubits shall be the height thereof: the horns thereof shall be of the same. And thou shalt overlay it with pure gold, the top thereof,

The Altar of Incense
(Uncovered and Partly Covered)

and the sides thereof round about, and the horns
thereof; and thou shalt make unto it a crown
of gold round about.   And two golden rings
shalt thou make to it under the crown of it,
by the two corners thereof, upon the two sides
of it shalt thou make it; and they shall be for
places for the staves to bear it withal.   And thou
shalt make the staves of acacia wood, and overlay
them with gold.   And thou shalt put it before
the veil that is by the ark of the testimony,
before the mercy seat that is over the testimony,
where I will meet with thee.   And Aaron shall
burn incense thereon, sweet incense of spices,
every morning: when he dresseth the lamps, he
shall burn incense upon it.   And when Aaron
lighteth the lamps at even, or between the two
evens, he shall burn incense upon it, a perpetual incense before the Lord throughout your
generations." (Exodus xxx. 1–8.)

"Incense, sweet incense!"   This tells the
preciousness of Christ ascended and accepted in
Himself and in all His work now in heaven;
gold and incense combine to give this altar its
name.   Opulent with Christ are the words which
describe it.   Aaron was to take a censer full of
burning coals of fire from off the altar before the
Lord, and his hands full of sweet incense beaten
small, and bring it within the veil, and bring it

once a year; this is Christ in the presence of
God for us. Again I say how blessed to look at
Him there and ourselves as one with Him! it
is Christ gone into heaven for us, where we are
holy—unblameable before God in love. Hence
this altar is for fellowship with the Father through
the Son. The glory inside was tempered by this
cloud of incense, and what the incense was to
Aaron, that the shrine of Christ's body was to
the effulgent brightness of the infinite glory; the
eye through Him could penetrate its loveliness
and admire its light. Without the cloud of incense Aaron could have no place before the glory
of God. He took it from off this golden altar
outside the curtains, and brought it before the
mercy-seat, over which the golden cherubim
spread their wings, and concerning which God
said, "There will I meet with thee"—the sweet
savour of the sacrifice and service of the Lord
Jesus as manifested by the incense, that Aaron
burnt on the altar morning and evening or
between the two evens.

In that incense and on that altar there was
no sin, no suffering, no remembrance of guilt;
only Christ Jesus—His excellence, His preciousness, His acceptance to God. Oh, blessed to
know that it is in His acceptance we are
accepted! in His excellence we are excellent

before God. Once a year Aaron had to go in where was the presence of the insufferable glory. But how, with an undazzled eye, could he look upon it? Never at meridian day with open face can we gaze at the sun, yet with what ease and admiration do we look on the planetory orbs as they softly shine down upon our world! It is the sun's light we see, though we see not the sun himself: it is *his* glory we behold. God is light insufferable, no man hath seen God at any time; too vast, too effulgent, too infinite is He to see. "The only begotten of the Father, He hath revealed Him."

Now this is not simply being at the cross, blessed as it is to be there; we cannot make too much of the cross; the cross is at the foundation of all our blessedness; this is Christ Himself. Some have so large a sense of themselves and their sins that they think more of them than of Christ. One great feature of the apostacy is, that it keeps the sinner at the crucifix, consequently they are always outside at the brazen altar, and seem to be perfect strangers to the peace, the rest, the joy, the assurance, and the light, of the golden altar. A risen, ascended, accepted Jesus for us at the Throne and in the presence of God, and ourselves counted by God as He is, appears to be quite unknown.

This Altar speaks of the old creation judicially gone, and Christ risen and accepted in its place. This we are saying over and over again, as never to be lost sight of; it will be Bunyan's Christian without his roll if we do. The scene is at the veil, it is the calm of heaven; God is here; the blood-speaking peace is here; sweet incense, the golden censer, is here, and we may come boldly. Before sin, God's throne was only one of glory; none could approach it but with veiled face. When sin came in, that throne to man became one of judgment: who could approach it boldly? but Christ did approach it, and received our doom for sin. Now it is all changed; the throne of judgment has now become a throne of grace; we come with unveiled face to it; yea, we come "boldly to obtain mercy, and find grace to help in every time of need." This is what the worshipper is entitled to enjoy—nay, to be in— as the ground and right of acceptance; it is here, on looking back, my sins seem all beset with grace.

But, as with all the other types, there is a perfect crowding of precious truths. The "acacia wood" tells of His incorruptible humanity, it is the shadow, the substance of which we read in Psalm xvi.: "Thou wilt not leave my soul in hell; neither wilt Thou suffer Thine Holy One to see corruption. Thou wilt show me the path of life : in Thy presence is fulness of joy ; at Thy right hand there are pleasures for evermore." How simple ! grand ! so unlike the poor thought of the ancients, who believed that the destruction of the body was fatal to all hopes of a continual existence after death. They embalmed their dead, as the only one thing they could do to show their love to their dear departed.

Then, besides the acacia wood and the gold, there is surmounting the altar

A CROWN OF GOLD

" round about." The kingliness as well as priest-liness. The Lord Jesus Christ, as He will be seen in the coming kingdom, as Ruler ("the God of the whole earth") and " Possessor of heaven and earth." Dispensationally, it is the Melchisedec order we see here ; in principle, it is applicable to us who know Him as raised from the dead crowned with glory and honour, and soon to be King and Head, with all things that now oppose put under His feet.

It was on this lovely heavenly scene, that the light from the sevenfold candlestick diffused its soft glories over each work of gold and tint and hue of those divinely-devised curtains.

What discoveries are these ! how easily discernible! coming from Christ as honey from the honeycomb. O Lord, how shall I praise Thee? I cannot burn with the glow of a David, but I must praise Thee whilst I have my being. Here in this Holy Place, Father, I will praise Thy name, oh, Thou Most High!

> "Worthy of homage, Lord, Thou art!
>   Such I would offer to Thee now,
>   The praise and worship of a heart
>   That only can in silence bow.
>
> " Here all the world that round me lies
>   Grows dim and distant to my view;
>   Upon *Thyself* I fix my eyes—
>   Sole object for the heart that's true.
>
> " Henceforth, while living for Thee here,
>   And linked *with* Thee in heaven above,
>   I'd walk as one whose heart holds dear
>   The memory of Thy matchless love."

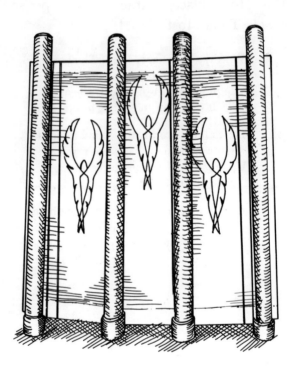

The Veil

7

The Veil

"The veil, that is to say, His flesh."—Hebrews 10:20

A ND now we come to the veil itself, beyond
which more glories await us. It separated
the holy from the most holy place, and, we know,
was so especially a type of Christ. Whilst the
veil was there it was a barrier in the way to the
holiest, none of the priests entered, and Aaron
only once a year. To the ordinary worshipper the
holiest was never manifest—the way of access was
not open. On the great day of atonement the
veil was raised for Aaron, who, with his white
ashes, entered into the holiest. A golden vessel
was in his hand with its cloud of incense. We are
not at a loss to know what the veil was ; the
apostle speaks of the veil of Christ's flesh. Some-
one has said, " The veil was the flesh of Christ,
that flesh which concealed God in His holiness
of judgment, in His perfectness as sovereign justice

itself." The Tabernacle was formed of the same materials as the Veil—figurative, as some suppose, of His own divine graces; others, of the grace of the Spirit in His redeemed people. May we not, as we have said, see it as the veil of His flesh—the Lord's human nature?

The construction of the Veil commands our notice. It was of fine-twined linen, embroidered with blue, scarlet, and purple; these represent the revealed human nature of Christ. They said, "This is what I am."

The white denoted *His holiness*, His righteousness, His intrinsic human perfectness; yea, the perfectness of His flesh which was conceived, not in sin or shapen in iniquity as with us, the fallen children of a fallen and corrupt ancestry, but of the Holy Ghost. Holy, harmless, undefiled, and separate from sinners was the blessed God-man—tempted in all points as we are, yet without sin.

Then the blue—*the heavenly*. Oh, how heavenly! in His pre-existence, in His character, His mission, His spirit. So that, as if He never had left heaven, He could say, "The Son of man, who also is in heaven."

Then, besides the white and the blue, there was the red—*atonement;* and, if the Hebrew expositors are right, the blood itself was on the Veil—on

Him and on us, one with Him, as cherubims with veil. That sprinkled blood tells of all heaven, glory, immortality, and eternal life being ours.

Then finally the purple, the *royal* colour, is a mixture of the blue and red. If not heavenly, and if no atoning blood, Christ could not have the kingdom, the dominion, or the glory. Blessed be His name, He is all we need, or that ever man, or angel, or God Himself could conceive. As the Veil was a wondrous piece of art, its lovely embroidery, and its varied hues, so the blessed Lord ; His "body was curiously wrought in the lower parts of the earth," and is now in heavenly beauty and glory. Peter said, "We were eye-witnesses of His *Majesty*."

The historical fact of the rending of the Veil must have been known to the ministering priests, and through them to the Levites, the high priest, and others. And *could* they, *did* they, deny it ? For the priest officiating in the evening sacrifice to see the Veil from the top, where no hand could reach, rent down to the bottom, was quite enough for him ever to deny or to forget it. What was it less than a miracle? especially as, according to Jewish writers, it was in substance three fingers thick. It was no less a supernatural event than the rocks rent asunder, the dead raised, and the One who was nailed to the accursed tree living, and seen by many infallible witnesses after His resurrection from the dead.

It is a day of unbelief. But did any who knew disbelieve this at the time? The five hundred that saw the risen Christ believed it. The three thousand and the four thousand converted under Peter believed it. They of Asia, and in Rome, to whom Paul preached, believed it. What has been discovered since to set aside the grounds of their belief of this fact, which, like the rocks of ages, showing their immovableness and un-changeableness by the waves that rise and break fruitlessly upon them, remains untouched and undeniable?

Let us not forget our own association with this phenomenon. "Cherubims" were wrought into the veil; they were one with it, one with Christ; we have been crucified with Him; dead with Christ, we are now as He is, risen and seated in heavenly places in Christ Jesus; what rest ineffable this gives! "Being myself one with Christ," says Luther, "all is peace: seeing myself in myself, I am as one who is lost."

That there is no veil to faith now we know from Hebrews x. 19, R.V.: "Having therefore, brethren, boldness to enter into the holy place by the blood of Jesus, by the way which He dedicated for us, a new and living way, *through the veil*, that is to say

His flesh." No longer an obstacle, the way is now an open way. That the veil was Christ is of easy understanding; our sins, our circumstances, and ourselves, all came between us and God ; they were the barriers which Christ undertook to bear away, and He bore them in His own body on the tree, and put them away by the sacrifice of Himself. By His death, sin and our fallen circumstances are now no more between us and God ; there is no sin on Christ, and none on us; He has taken it away, and left the kingdom of heaven open to all believers. Hence now, as Aaron was on the great day of the atonement, we are "made nigh through the blood of Christ." He was before God once a year, because the blood was there. We are before God continuously because Christ is there ; we have not to be made nigh, or to cry "nearer," we are as near as Christ. It is now with " open face" we see the glory of the Lord, it is with "boldness" (liberty) we have access to God, and in such sense we are never out of the sanctuary ; it is our true scene of worship ; we are never absent worshippers. This is our place as God sees us ; in our ignorance, or sin, we may not live in the power of it, or enjoy as we might, its blessedness. Sin, death, and hell were all between us and God ; they are so no more ; the rending of the veil, *i.e.*, Christ's flesh, His death, put them all away.

Need more be said ? " This veil, now removed, was suspended on its appointed pillars, four in number," suggested the late Mr. Soltau, who has written largely and blessedly on the Tabernacle, " wisdom, righteousness, sanctification, and redemption."   It was in the days of Aaron, between the Holy and Most Holy Places ; and along with him, as it were, by faith we may enter and survey the grand surprising mysteries that await us there.

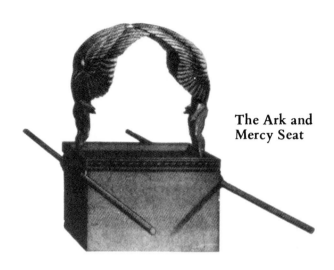

The Ark and Mercy Seat

The Ark and Mercy Seat Partly Covered

8

The Most Holy Place

"And after the second veil, the tabernacle which is called the holiest of all; which had the golden censer, and the art of the covenant overlaid round with gold, wherein was the golden pot that had manna, and Aaron's rod that budded, and the tables of the covenant; and over it the cherubims of glory shadowing the mercy-seat."—Hebrews 9:3-5

THE "hush" we felt on entering the Holy Place is intensified here. It is truly God's *"dwelling* place ;" it is His *" secret* place." " There will I meet with thee," are words which indicate its true meaning. The blessed challenge God gives of meeting with us is not now for the putting away of sins, or providing against wrath, but for fellowship, for holiest and happiest communion with Himself. It is our sweet home now ; we are there by faith. Oh, love and grace ineffable ! " being justified by faith, we have peace with God through our Lord Jesus Christ : by whom also we have access by faith into this grace wherein we stand."

THE ARK OF THE COVENANT,

or "*secret of His presence*," is the only object in this place. It is inside the curtain; that is, the veil, solitary and alone. Small in itself, yet it has its several parts, each one full of divine truth; and shows more than any other that for which the Tabernacle was made; viz., the dwelling-place of the Most High. This small chest—only about four feet and four inches long, two feet and seven inches wide, and two feet and seven inches deep —was made of acacia wood, and covered over with pure gold. The blood brought in from outside the camp told of Christ's death; the acacia wood foreshadowed His incorruption; though He died, death did not hold Him; He saw no corruption. How precious this! "Because I live," said Christ, "ye shall live also." His resurrection is seen in

AARON'S ROD

that was laid up in the ark, and which, contrary to all nature, budded and bore fruit. Could anything be more dead or hopeless of life than a stick without root, and without connection with earth or air? Could anyone be more dead than One who lay a day and two nights in the heart of the earth? one moment dead would have been enough for atonement, but such a time showed to His enemies the reality of His death. Taken down from the Tree, "What an end of Him!" may the priests who hated Him have said. "Ah!" they thought, "no more our place and nation in danger."

Beside the rod there was the golden pot that had

MANNA—

"angels' food," on which God in the wilderness fed the millions of His people. The bread was from heaven, and symbolized Him who could say, "I am the bread of life;" and again, "He that eateth of the bread that I shall give him shall never hunger."

I have said it is called the Ark of the testimony. The testimony represented the law; the law in the hands of Moses became broken—prophetic of how it was and would be with man. Christ was the only One who ever perfectly kept it, there was no fault in Him; He could say, "Thy law have I hid in My heart."

The Lord's Bible was of three parts—the books of Moses, the Prophets, and the Psalms; from these He gave exposition of the Word relating to Himself; whilst on His way to Emmaus "He opened up to them the Scriptures," showing how perfect was His belief in Moses, and in the writings ascribed to him, to which He again and again referred. God's thought in the demands of the law was not that man would keep it, for He knew what was in man, and that a corrupt nature could never produce a holy life. It is a glass which exposes man's spiritual deformity and short-coming; moreover, it brings in the whole race guilty, that every mouth may be stopped, and that salvation may be of grace. Some speak of it as the rule of life, and surely a rule it is by which we may judge of ourselves; but Christ Himself is our only true rule of life.

THE MERCY-SEAT

was a slab of gold, forming the top of the Ark. The term "Mercy-seat"—the seat of mercy, or mercy at rest—signifies propitiation, the root idea of which is *covering*. David understood this, "Blessed is the man whose sin is covered." God put the cover marked with blood over the law, over sins the law had condemned. Because of the blood (death for sin) God can say, "I will not so much as see your sins, but will cover them;" this He has done in Christ; "He hath perfected for ever them that are sanctified." He died that, as far as the east is from the west, so far might He remove our transgressions from us; and as none could see the law, because of the Mercy-seat, so He sees not our transgression, because of Christ. It is as if God had said, "Look on those tables;

I will cover them in Christ." The covering was of pure gold, signifying the divine; also of acacia wood, the perfect incorruptible humanity; and on the covering was the blood. Thus the true Mercy-seat (Christ) was between God and our sins; some have called it "the fairest image of Christ." Sometimes the child of God has bemoaned himself thus, "What if after all I should be lost?" The devil would have you ever looking at yourself, and at the broken law, not upon Christ. The Mercy-seat shuts down all that could be against you, it says, "no condemnation to them that are in Christ." It is through knowing Christ, and not looking at self, that God can make us conquerors over sin and death. This, too, is our comfort and strength for communion, that God is satisfied. Poor soul, if the broken law be thy trouble, bring it to Calvary; if a guilty conscience, bring it to the blood.

I would add this, the Ark itself was of vast moment to Israel; we have been reminded how the feelings of the godly were regulated by it; when *it* was lost Eli fell from his seat and died, and his daughter-in-law named her child Ichabod; or, "Where is the glory?" When the Ark had gone, God seemed gone; Israel was without her true bulwark. Hence, when the Ark was brought back, David danced for joy before it. Everything else in Israel was as nothing compared with the joy unspeakable of God having come again into their midst. Some day we know the heavens will open, and it will be seen as if descending to earth again, to show that God, in the day of Jacob's trouble, will come to the help of His people. In the wilderness it abode inside the curtain; this will not be so in the day of the Lord. That which had been their joy of old will be their joy again—a joy surprising, unspeakable, and full of their promised glory.

We see a crown or cornice of massive gold surmounting it, and a border raised above the rest of the Ark, both for splendid adorning and for uniting the Mercy-seat to the ark. How parabolic of that peaceful time when all Christ's enemies shall be put under His feet, and He will reign King of kings, and Lord of lords!

Note the connection between the Mercy-seat and

THE CHERUBIM.

They are inseparable, made out of the same material—gold, forming one beautiful symbol. This reminds us Christ and His redeemed are all one, therefore He is not ashamed to call them brethren. A sweet word, comprehensive of all! we have read it in the book of the Psalms— "I will declare Thy name unto My brethren;" it was His resurrection word—"Go tell My brethren."

With such oneness and such relationship no marvel He is not ashamed. Not ashamed, because He that sanctifies and they that are sanctified are all (like the cherubim and the Mercy-seat) of one, or of one sort, as the word is.

Very delightful to call all this to mind, now that we are where these human faces of ineffable sweetness and blessedness are associated with the whole work and Person of Him who was our true propitiation. Calm is the majesty and the look of innocence in these cherubim; their faces are toward each other, with their eyes complacently intent on the atoning blood at their feet; their place is here in the Holiest and on the Mercy-seat. They see the reflected glory on a substance of pure gold; and gazing they receive the same, just as looking at Christ we become reflectors of His light. Tholuck thus speaks of himself:

> " Tender and soft my heart has grown,
>   Patient and kind to all ;
>   The rays from the bright model there
>   Upon the copy fall.
>
> " Here in my bosom all is calm,
>   No cares or passions move,
>   While drops from the eternal light
>   Fall gently from above."

These are heart-affecting wonders. There may be in the great pagan world shrines of gold and silver, and curtains of splendour, but where is the glory? where the supernatural glory of the living God? How poor the shrines of the so-called gods which are no gods—Moloch, Rimmon, Ashtaroth, and all the idols of Syria; Baal, Dagon, and all the false deities of Phœnicia; Apis, and all the monster deities of Egypt. Lift this veil, and what sweetness of beauty meets the eye! How one loves their calm manifestations!

We would here ask, as we are in the presence of the uncreated glory, and it is our home, How do we feel in such a place? *are we at home?* And this is heaven, it is the manifestation of our eternal home. Do we feel our right to be there amid the ineffable displays of God Himself, having full knowledge of the righteousness of God in Christ? What thousands of Christians, it is to be feared, know nothing of the enjoyment by faith of what God thus is, and of what fellowship is in His own very highest heavens.

Perhaps no study is more deeply interesting than the cherubim. There must be something of immense moment in the Divine Mind respecting them, for beside their being in this very highest heaven of God, and the place assigned them in the Temple, there is not a spot in the veil or the inner curtains of the Tabernacle that is not embroidered and beautified with them.

THEIR FORM

is one of beauty.   Artists and sculptors pride
themselves in their representations of " the human
face divine ; " but no art of man, no devising of
his highest genius, could, we believe, reach to the
Divine model such as we see here. He alone knew
what it prefigured, just as He alone knew what the
first pair in the garden prefigured—Christ and His
Church.   Who but He could tell the full meaning
of, " Let us make man in our image, after our likeness "—not only morally, but the likeness in bodily
form of what Christ now is ; not merely in His
incarnation as Son of man, but as " the altogether
lovely " ?

THEIR ATTITUDE

They stand on the Mercy-seat—at rest there
where the blood of the sacrifice had been sprinkled,
and where their heads, faces, yea, whole persons,
were covered with the glory in which they stood.

In the Tabernacle their faces were towards each
other, looking downward upon the blood ; they
could have looked nowhere else.   If they had
looked outward on the world, they would have
seen nothing but sin and sorrow ; if they had
looked on Israel, they would have seen a stiff-
necked people. Just as now, where can we look
for peace or rest ? If we look at *man*, sin, sickness,

death, and the grave are before us; if at *the world*, it is simply enmity with God; if at *self*, we see sin and defilement. The cherubim in the Holiest looked on Christ; blessed be His name, we do the same, and there alone our rest and peace are to be found. In the Temple, instead of being compara- tively small, as in the Tabernacle, they were two magnificent figures; their faces were not looking downwards but inwards; *i.e.*, into the ample space of the Temple. This they did because in the Solomon-day the whole earth will be filled with the glory of the Lord, and may well draw forth their admiring gaze. At home and at rest, as in their own magnificent place, they remind us of how "we all, with unveiled face reflecting as a mirror the glory of the Lord, are transformed into the same image from glory to glory even as from the Lord the Spirit." (R.V.) Thus are they in the presence of the Lord Himself, where is our own special place given us in Christ, with sin and self for ever put away.

THEIR NAME

What shall we say of it? and what have not others said of it? In Genesis iii. 23, as we shall see, it is one signifying "MADE TO DWELL"; we know "he that dwelleth in love dwelleth in God, and God in him." God had never so dwelt with the faultless ones in the garden, He had *visited*

them, *conversed* with them, *companied* them in
their walk; but He did not *dwell* with them.   Of
Enoch and Noah it is said, they "walked with
God," but He did not visibly dwell with them;
yet was there a growth of things—Abraham was
called the friend of God; and God again and
again talked with Him.   "Singularly lovely are
the visits he pays to Abraham."   But here is
something more than a visit.   "Made to dwell,"
suggestive not only of all that is social, but of
love indulging itself in its own elect object; so
that that which was foreshadowed at the gate of
the garden was formally announced to Moses.
What food for richest meditation is here!   Sweet
to hear God say, "let them," His own redeemed
people, "make Me a sanctuary; that I may dwell
among them."   And what a presence! obviously
of love and delight, as to Israel; and to us through
all the eternal days in which we are to be for ever
with Him.   How wondrous to gaze upon His past
wilderness delight, and in Israel's coming days to
hear Him say, renewing it again, "I will turn to
the people a pure language, that they may all call
upon the name of the Lord, to serve Him with
one consent."   Long estranged, but the estrange-
ment will be over then.   "From beyond the rivers
of Ethiopia," He says, "My suppliants, even the
daughter of My dispersed, shall bring Mine offering.

In that day shalt thou not be ashamed for all thy
doings, wherein thou hast transgressed against Me;
for then I will take away out of the midst of thee
them that rejoice in thy pride, and thou shalt no
more be haughty because of Mine holy mountain.
. . . The remnant of Israel shall not do iniquity
. . . they shall feed and lie down, and none shall
make them afraid . . . THE LORD THY GOD IN
THE MIDST OF THEE is mighty; He will save,
*He will rejoice over thee with joy; He will rest
in His love, He will joy over thee with singing.*"

It is now the rest, broken in the wilderness and
in Canaan, will be more than renewed. We know
as to ourselves God says, "Ye are the temple of
the living God; as God hath said, I will dwell in
them, and walk in them; and I will be their God,
and they shall be My people." Oh, wonderful that
God deigns to do this, and that we are privileged
to dwell with Him! Yes, with *Him;* not a mere
abstraction which clouds our comprehension, but a
living One, infinite in grace and love. And further,
"simple personality merely would not constitute a
Being fitted to attract us; mere power, for example,
might awe, but could not command our love. The
creation of the heavens and the earth imply con-
sciousness, but there is the still grander disclosure
of a moral character in the Divine approval as at
the first of the things made, which He said were

'*good*,' in the beneficence which provides for the happiness of all living things, and above all in the requirement from mankind of obedience to a sovereign standard of right, in the will of a holy and benevolent Creator." This is seen in the first pages of the Word, but it is in His Son fully revealed we see God is love.

I need not say that there are many

DIVERSIFIED VIEWS

on this subject of the cherubim. "The cherubim," says Dr. Andrew Bonar, "foreshadowed redeemed men amid the trees of Eden restored—the type of the Church dwelling in the Lord's presence, revelling (so to speak) in divine mysteries." They were first seen at the garden of Eden, occupying the hallowed spot where the tree of life waved its branches. Leviticus, and these descriptions in Exodus, are but the expansion of this scene in the garden. Another, who has written well on this, in his beautiful work on Leviticus, says, "The cherubim throughout the Old Testament, wherever they act, are connected with the judicial power of God . . . and belong to the Throne. Here God manifested Himself as the supreme God in His moral being, armed with power to enforce respect to His laws, and to keep account of all that was done. This is also why the blood witnesses of all that had been done for those who had thus been responsible, and, satisfying all the moral nature of Him who sat there, was put upon the Mercy-seat. Thence came forth the communication to Moses, 'And I will commune with thee from above the mercy-seat, from between the two cherubim which are upon the ark of the testimony.'" *

Deeply interested am I in the charming view taken by another dear man of God. †

"I have taken a good deal of trouble in searching into the works which learned men have written upon this subject. It is very remarkable what opposite views they have taken. Some have said they were the same as the cherubim described in Ezekiel i., and that they were also the same as the four living ones mentioned in Rev. iv., also that they were representations of Deity, of the attributes of God, and that in connection with the incarnation of the Lord Jesus Christ there was seen the face of a man. It appears to me there are most serious objections to this view. I do not think that God anywhere warrants us in supposing there could be any representation of Deity. It is a curious fact that whether from tradition or from other sources, heathen nations learned to make deities after the pattern of those winged creatures. Some of them may be seen in the British Museum,

---

* *Synopsis of the Books of the Bible.*   † KRAUSE.

though perhaps I should not have said they were heathen deities, because no one knows what they were. But, again, others have imagined the cherubim were representations of angels; they have said the relation which was to subsist between these holy beings and man was here shadowed forth. I have the same objection to this view that I have to the other. I shall now tell you the view I take of the subject, though I plainly acknowledge I have not one particle of authority for it in the Word of God. I would remind you of the first place in Scripture where we read of the cherubim. It has been thought by some that this passage presents the chief difficulty; to me it appears to explain the whole matter. You remember that when man was driven out of paradise the Lord 'placed at the east of the garden of Eden cherubims, and a flaming sword which turned every way to keep the way of the tree of life,' the ordinary interpretation of which passage is this: that the Lord placed angels as sentinels to keep man *from approaching* the tree of life, from which, by his transgression, he had been excluded. Some of our most learned critics have found great fault with the translation of the passage, and I think most justly. I shall read it according to the translation they have given. 'So He drove out the man, and He TABERNACLED at the east of the

garden of Eden WITH CHERUBIM; AND A GLIT-
TERING FLICKERING FLAME' (it is impossible to
translate the word exactly) 'TURNED EVERY WAY
TO KEEP THE WAY ABOUT THE TREE OF LIFE.'
The word here translated '*tabernacled*' is the same
as that from which the word '*tabernacle*,' so often
used in the book of Exodus, comes.   It is *the root
of the word 'shekina,' that very glory which appeared
between the cherubim.* The view this translation gives
me is this, that though man was driven out of the
garden of Eden, God still preserved the way of the
tree of life.   But how did He do it?   He tabernacled
Himself with men, His elect and believing people.
He tabernacled Himself in their midst as this bright
and glittering flame, preserving the way to the tree
of life, and preserving them to Himself.   This view
of the passage in Genesis iii. supplies a key to the
understanding of the subject. I regard the cherubim
as a representation of the whole elect people of
God.   And when I come to Exodus xxv., and see
that within the holy place from which the people
were excluded were these figures of the great truth
that God would dwell with man, then I say I
can understand how from eternity it has been
God's great purpose that He would bring His own
redeemed people into that place of His presence,
into which others have no entrance at all."

This rendering to me is truly beautiful, and of

deep interest. According to it, the flickering, glittering sword—the same as the Shekinah—represents God. The Tree of life we know is Christ ; and the cherubim, which signify " made to dwell," represent man, who, though just driven because of sin away from that Tree, now has access to it through Christ, who is the Righteousness of God. And it seems as if God, who had driven him out on the one ground, was delighted on the other to restore and enjoy him, even to give him to dwell with Himself.

It is remarkable that the cherubim were part and parcel of the Mercy-seat itself, made out of the same slab of pure gold, as Christ and His own " are all of one." In Exodus xxxvii. we read, " And he made two cherubims of gold, beaten out of one piece made he them, on the two ends of the mercy-seat ; one cherub on the end on this side ; and another cherub on the other end on that side : out of the mercy-seat made he the cherubims on the two ends thereof. And the cherubims spread out their wings on high, and covered with their wings over the mercy-seat, with their faces one to another ; even to the mercy-seatward were the faces of the cherubims." And it is remarkable also that the cherubims were rent together with the veil, answering to Galatians, in which we are said to be crucified with Christ.

One who has spent his life over the Word * remarks, "The four living ones in Rev. iv. represent

"THE CHURCH IN RESURRECTION GLORY,

"as God's agency for earth and heaven, for time and
for eternity, 'the fulness of Him that filleth all in
all.' The whole company of the redeemed in
heavenly and eternal glory are symbolized by the
two large cherubim in the most holy place of the
Temple of Solomon. (1 Kings vi. 23–28 ; 2 Chron.
iii. 10–13.) They are formed of 'olive tree' or
oil wood, emblematic of the spiritual bodies of
the redeemed ; of 'image work,' as conformed
to the image of the living Christ ; covered with
'gold,' as partakers of a glory which is divine.
Their wings reach from wall to wall, filling all
heaven, according to the will of God, with the
knowledge of His truth, and with the manifestation
of His glory." The same author speaks thus of

THE CHARIOT OF THE CHERUBIM :

"God, who as the Creator and Upholder of all
things employs the innumerable company of angels
as His chariot or vehicle of communication with
the subjects of His vast empire throughout the
universe, will also, as universal Father, employ in
His sovereign grace the redeemed in resurrection
glory, and in spiritual bodies, as His chariots or

* Mr. Newberry in his valuable translation of the Bible.

vehicles of communication with the children of His vast family. And as the wings of the cherubim met in the centre of the holiest, immediately over the blood-stained propitiatory of the ark, even so redemption through the blood of the Lamb will be the centre theme of the testimony borne by the redeemed to the utmost bounds of creation; for God, who has headed up all things in Christ, hath also reconciled all things to Himself, through the blood of His cross, 'whether they be things on earth, or things in heaven;' so that the myriads of angels, and every creature throughout the universe, may join in the song which ascribes 'blessing and honour, and glory and power, unto Him that sitteth upon the throne.'" This is grand, and we may truly say—

> " That which was strangest thing of all,
>   At first seemed e'en for babes too small;
>   And yet at length so vast it grows,
>   As if all heaven it would enclose."

Who that wants to know what our own sweetest portion in heaven will be, let them look once more at these cherubim, how in the midst of the glory they look directly on Christ. The promise to us is—

" THEY SHALL SEE HIS FACE,"

as if all heaven were concentrated there. It means, first, ineffable *nearness*. Poor Balaam said, "I shall see Him, but not now: I shall behold Him, but

not nigh." The happy near vision will be for His
own, we shall see Him in His beauty; and, secondly,
it supposes *a complete moral capacity*—we shall see
the face of God and live. What holiness! what
purity! The natural man receiveth not the things
which be of God; and if he could see Him there
would be no delight, no joy. Oh, the blessedness
of a Divine nature, a nature according to all that
God is, as He will be seen in the face of Jesus
Christ! It supposes, thirdly, *perpetuity of delight.*
This is a favourite chord on the harp of the poets.

> " There shall I see His face,
>   And never, never sin ;
> And from the rivers of His grace
>   Drink endless pleasures in." *

> " Oh for the hour of seeing
>   My Saviour face to face—
> The hope of ever being
>   In that sweet meeting-place !" †

> " How shall I meet those eyes?
>   Mine on Himself I cast,
> And own myself the Saviour's prize—
>   Mercy from first to last." ‡

> " In the radiance of the glory
>   First I saw His blessed face,
> And for ever shall that glory
>   Be my home, my dwelling-place." §

> "We know Him as we could not know
>   Through heaven's golden years ;
> We there shall see His glorious face,
>   But Mary saw His tears." §

---

* WATTS.   † Mrs. BANCROFT.   ‡ MONTGOMERY.   § Mrs. BEVAN.

And seeing Him, we shall see all else we need—
heaven, bright heaven and its bliss, the earth,
not as now, but in its true glory.   Yes, a day, a
morning without clouds.

> "And with the morn, those angel faces smile,
>   Which we have loved long since, and lost awhile."

There is something intensely interesting in the
thought of

THE SHEKINAH OR VISIBLE GLORY.

It is as if God said, "I am here, I am with you."
We know He is everywhere in all worlds, with all
beings and all things which He hath created ; but
where is there anything like this, whether in heaven
or on earth—God so dwelling with us ?   What a
spectacle !   An obviously supernatural and visible
object ; God in mystic form of a bright attendant
cloud—Patron, Friend, Guide, Protector, and Lover ;
just so familiar with Israel in the wilderness,
always with them, even when, as we have said,
for their sin they had to turn back.   A specimen
this of, " I will never leave thee, nor forsake
thee."   " This glory," says another, " had guided
them from the first, and had set up its throne of
power in their midst.   It had judged Pharaoh and
his legions to the deep, and had smitten the
nations of Canaan, dividing the land for Israel
His inheritance, having His Throne and Temple in

Jerusalem. He did not seek any other spot on
earth; but being disturbed at Jerusalem by the
defilements there, He returned to heaven. (Ezek. xi.)
From thence in due season He came back, yet in
another form. But He had a special character in
which to show Himself—one equally worthy of
itself—I mean in the form and character of grace.
Accordingly this same glory or divine presence—
God Himself—returned veiled in the Person of
Jesus; and as a rejected Galilean, a carpenter's son,
not having where to lay His head, went about in the
land of Israel in fullest grace—healing, preaching,
toiling, watching; poor, yet enriching others;
thirsting and hungering, yet feeding thousands;
and in everything as simply and surely declaring
itself to be the glory, as it did when it divided
the waters of Jordan or threw down the walls of
Jericho. But in this form Israel, or the earth,
forfeited it also, though it did not leave the earth
in the same way. Of old, when rejected in its
power, it left the earth of itself, in righteous anger
resenting the affront done to its majesty, and with-
drawing itself in judgment. (Ezekiel i.–xi.) But
now, being rejected in its grace, it remains still to
bless the earth, if haply man would own the love,
and is at last rather sent away than withdraws
itself. But still, whether we see the glory in power
or in grace, the earth for the time has forfeited it,

for He is still unchangeable, and it is now hid in
the heavens.   But there is another stage in its
history still.   Ezekiel sees it returning to the very
spot from whence it set out.   It had, as said, never
sought any other place on earth.   If Zion be un-
prepared for the glory they must lose it, for of
Zion alone has He said, ' This is My rest for ever ;'
but the glory does return, as we see in that chapter
in Ezekiel.   And then will arise the system com-
monly known as the millennium, when Jesus will
become the centre, the true ladder which Jacob
saw, the Sustainer of all things in heaven and in
earth, having now reconciled all by His blood, and
then gathering all in Himself, to spread His divers
glories over all. " *   Nor the millennium alone, as
we have seen ; near the Tree of life, before dispensations, was this self-same glory.   That Tree is
Christ ; blessed prospect ! all who believe will have
right to the Tree of life, and will enter in through
the gates (millennial or eternal) into the city.

And now to go back to the Holiest.   He who is
splendour-loving should study this scene, what
the glory here is who can tell ? what, upon the
Mercy-seat, where was received and reflected the
glory ?   It will be our portion for ever to see
Christ, and what spectators ! how delightful even
now to think how the Mary-mother, and the

* J. G. B.

other Mary so early at His sepulchre, are ineffably happy seeing Him as He is; and Peter, James, and John, and the faithful who were with Him in His temptation. Can we conceive of what it is their being as they are with Him, and all believers from their time down—many of whose names we love so well—these too are there, and all whose names are written in the Lamb's Book of Life.

But how awful the thought suggested by Wesley, "What if my name should be left out!" What a forfeit to fall short of this heaven! Do we now by faith breathe freely as we walk about these courts of the Lord's house? Do we see the Lord, and live happy in His love? for, to have heaven there, we must carry it in the heart here.

And now retracing our ground—

> "Sweet is the harp of prophecy—too sweet
> Not to be wronged by a mere mortal touch :
> Nor can the wonders it records be sung
> To meaner music and not suffer loss."

For what is it all, as displayed by Moses, but a foretelling of the whole great system God had in His mind for glorifying Himself, exalting Christ, and lifting up man from the lowest depths of his degradation to the highest heights of glory. And now we close here, calling to mind the words of the sweet singer, "How amiable [lovely] are Thy tabernacles, O Lord of hosts!" in that psalm

of the Divine Presence to which thousands have
bent their meditative gaze, finding away from all
earthly cares or alarms their needed security and
rest in God.   Blessed psalmist! some imagine that
the Old Testament saints had no such free access
to God.   Not the writer here?   Not Moses, who
had face to face communion with the divine glory?
Not Abraham?   No, what is said is, that "the
way into the holiest was not yet made *manifest*,"
as it now is, since Christ came, who has revealed
to us the Father.   Not access to God!   The saints
of old—Joseph, Daniel, Jeremiah?   Oh, would
that of God's children more were as these—as
Enoch, who walked with God, or David, the man
after God's own heart, or Abraham His friend.

Cowper says of some natural scene—

> "The calm retreat, the silent shade
> With prayer and praise agree."

But what may we not say of this scene for
fellowship with God in the secret place of the
Most High!

> "Both seem by Thy sweet beauty made
> For those who follow Thee."

It is here we have security: "I will say of the
Lord, He is my refuge and my fortress: my God;
in Him will I trust."

Sweet thoughts.   Covered with the feathers of

the Almighty, as bird under the wings of the mother bird. All this by faith now, no cold, no fear, no foreboding of ill. These feathers show God's providing love, His faithful love, His tender love, His protecting love—how He delights in feeling us near! Oh, why should we ever doubt, or get separate from Him into the cold of the world! The little bird responds to the uplifted wing, nor doubts its welcome. If we want to love God more, we must think more of such love as this; for it is true here, " We love Him because He first loved us." Moreover, it is this love which conquers us, and which leads us away captive from all our embarrassments, entanglements, and fearfulnesses, making us conquerors over the sins of the flesh and the spirit, and our love of a world perishing with its using. As with the bird so with us; we break away from all obstacles, and rest under the shadow of His wings.

According to the psalm, angels have charge; the lion and adder of hell tread not here. No sound of the outer griefs or the altar sorrows; it is rest, perfect rest. You understand, or do you not understand? for it is the heritage now of every one that believeth. Not practical? Who that knows the place but must bring its atmosphere into all the details of practical life, walking *with* God.

9

The Rings and Staves

"And thou shalt makes staves of shittim wood, and overlay them with gold. And thou shalt put the staves into the rings by the sides of the ark, that the ark may be borne with them. The staves shall be in the rings of the ark: they shall not be taken from it."—Exodus 15:13-15

THESE were common to many of the sacred vessels of the Sanctuary; the brazen and golden altars; the ark of the testimony, the table of shewbread, all had their appointed staves and rings. Not only is Christ divine, but He must be made known in a divine way: He would not allow a demon to testify, but rebuked him. Only such as God calls can serve Him; the apostles must tarry at Jerusalem until endued with power from on high; *i.e.*, until heaven, as it were, is come down to be with them. This makes it a solemn act—professed service for the Lord Jesus Christ. The fact is, the ark had to be carried from place to place, and these were the instruments, just as, suggestively, Christ has to be evangelised from place to place. A child could put his hand to these staves. Many a father, mother, sister, or brother have been awakened by the living or dying testimony of one young in years and young in grace. Our work is to itinerate Christ, to carry about the proclamation of Jesus and the resurrection : that was the doctrine which confounded or converted. The apostles went everywhere telling, as did Mary, "The Lord is risen ;" Paul delighted to prove it, to the Jews first and also to the Gentiles. "And," said he, "if Christ be not raised, ye are yet in your sins ;" of course, if there be no risen One, all else fails.

I have found that preaching Christ's death is what a soul sick of sin needs ; but preaching resurrection, where all sins are lost sight of for ever, is what gives peace, and assurance ; for the Holy Ghost witnesseth (because of Christ's death and resurrection), "Their sins and their iniquities will I remember no more." Blessed words! how sweet they sound in the ear of faith now! what music by-and-by, should the Lord tarry, in the cold, dull ear of death! Oh, ye ministers of Christ, *preach the Word!* tell of His dying love! proclaim His risen power! Yes, His *risen* power ; for here is the grand keystone of the whole Arch of a true Christianity ; remove it, and the entire fabric falls. But what mouth of man or devil ever silenced the five hundred that were eye-witnesses of Him after His resurrection? or what human or

infernal power could ever displace that Angel that
sat in such quiet triumph upon the rolled-away
stone of the sepulchre ?   The very Lord's-day is a
monument to the infidel of what *he* asserts never
happened, and was never known in history.

Let the five "Alls" be the true lines on which
the evangelist shall work when his hands are upon
these altar staves, and he carries Christ to the
dying sons of men.

First, "*All* the world."   This is where the
Church is to go, but has never yet gone, after
nearly two thousand years.   Second, "*All* power."
It is ours to carry the ark, to tell of Christ; it is
His to make it the power of God unto salvation.
It has always been a comfort to me that I have no
responsibility further than the message.   To give
life is all His own work.   The grain of wheat has
died ; the abiding *alone* will never be, fruit, in the
salvation of many, will follow.   But how will the
fruit come ? by what power will the harvest be
plentiful and golden ?   The answer brings us to
our third "all."   He Himself tells us, " I, if I be
lifted up, will draw *all* unto Myself." (R.V.)   And
again, "All that the Father hath given Me shall
come to Me ; and him that cometh I will in
no wise " (on no consideration) "cast out."   And
fourthly, " *all* things."   We are to declare all
things, whatsoever He hath declared.   Not some,
but all.   Doctrine, precept, promise, prophecy,
the purposes and the dispensations, the whole

counsel of God; and this in season and out of season. And fifthly, "*All* the days." Yes; now, as in days past, will He, whose work it is, be with the labourer. He says, "Lo, I am with you *all the days*." In days of brightness or of gloom; in days of peace or enmity of many; in days of life or death, the same, "*I* am with you!" He was with Daniel in the lions' den. He was with Jeremiah in the pit, with David in exile, with John in the little Patmos isle, with Paul and Silas in their prisons, with Stephen in his martyrdom, with Huss and Jerome in the fire, with Allen Gardiner dying in a famine, with Marshman, Carey, Williams, Moffat, and the thousands of others who have gone forth in His Name, and have hazarded their lives for His Name's sake. Whole lands are yet unreached, some not discovered. Our consolation is not one of a heartless orthodoxy, as if resting on our oars whilst a drowning age lay all around us; but in the midst of much failure we rest in that truth of God which says, "I give unto them [My sheep] eternal life, and they shall never perish." Many another precious truth may suggest itself at these altars, but they say to us:

"Shall we whose souls are lighted with wisdom from on high,
    Shall we to man benighted the lamp of life deny?"

**The High Priest of Israel on the
Great Day of Atonement**

10

The High Priesthood of the Tabernacle

"Seeing then that we have a great High Priest, that is passed into the heavens, Jesus, the Son of God, let us hold fast our profession."—Hebrews 4:14

THERE were millions in Israel, but only one as high priest walked these courts; just as now there are millions of the saints in heaven and on earth, but only One is our precious High Priest, and we want none other. He is all our salvation and all our desire.

Who that makes himself a priest to offer sacrifices is guilty of a profane and awful usurpation of the Name and offices of Christ.

The priestly and the kingly come to mind. Aaron is as the Lord: we get a wonderful sense of what Christ as Priest is now doing from what Aaron did. For why was Aaron taken from among men, but that he may offer sacrifices for sins? This was his special work; this also Christ has done, having offered Himself. Aaron was to bear gently with the ignorant and the erring, who often came with their griefs and their guilt into the outer court, as we have seen. This *He* did who would not break a bruised reed, nor quench the smoking flax. Aaron took not the honour on himself, but was called of God; so also Christ; He glorified not Himself to be made an High Priest, but He that spake unto Him, "Thou art my Son, this day have I begotten Thee;" the result being that He is the author of eternal salvation to them that obey Him. The high priest was one who was gentle and lowly in himself; this the blessed Saviour was; and we, poor ignorant and erring sinners, are the objects of His care. Of course, in His character and perfectness also in His work Christ goes far beyond Aaron; Aaron offered often, the Lord but once. Aaron, by reason of death, was only one of a succession of priests; the Lord *ever* lives, and will never have a successor, nor hand over our cause to another; He will never leave the mercy-seat till all His blood-bought ones are brought in.

But He was beyond Aaron as Priest for ever after, the beautiful rims of the altar in the form of crowns told of far more than we see in Aaron; these give glimpses of Christ being a King as well as a Priest. Having expiated our sins, He will reign, and we with Him, over the earth.

The cherubim were on a throne. " Him that overcometh will sit with Me in My Throne, even as I am set down with My Father in His Throne." The holiest has no suffering in it ; in the coming glory all is rest ; righteousness alone will reign. Crowned with a crown of thorns again He will never be ; crowned with glory and honour He now is. Hence all this lovely serenity in the Holy and Most Holy places, God delighting to pourtray His own beloved Son. The golden altars and their crowns, the cherubim and precious stones, indicate peace and joy and rest. Aaron's attire suggests the glory of Christ's Person as " chiefest among ten thousand, and altogether lovely." The world will not be always as it is ; this fair gem, plucked from its Owner by the hand of Satan, and for ages under his deceiving, darkening, and desolating rule, will be wrested from his possession, and made to adorn the brow of its rightful Sovereign and King.

The scene of Aaron's ministry was inside the Tabernacle, as the scene of Christ's Priesthood is inside the heavens. Atonement was made outside the camp just as Christ's death for us was here on earth. To make atonement there was death, but for priesthood Christ ever lives. The death was once for all, but the priesthood continues, and will continue until all are brought home to Himself.

Paul, in his epistle to the Hebrews, shows how no man could be a priest on earth, but one of the tribe of Levi; and our Lord, says the apostle, sprang out of *Judah,* and was therefore Himself never a priest on earth. It is well to know this, and to regulate our worship accordingly and in spirit, ourselves to be where He is, and know our meetness for the scene. The altar and Sanctuary are in heaven; there too by grace we are purged worshippers, made nigh through the blood. Many, professedly worshipping, think only of some earthly scene, and rise no higher than the place where they are; others are ever praying that they *may* draw near.

We have seen the Tabernacle, the dwelling-place of God, the wondrous details of its inward glory and external mien, as representing Christ and His people; we can only point to these things; each heart must unlock for itself the marvellous wealth and fulness that are hidden in them.

We are now dwelling for a little upon

THE PRIESTHOOD,

instituted by God for its service.

For such an office to represent God's own Son, and for such a work to deal with the sins of the people, appearing for them when put away, in the very presence of God which we have sought

to describe in the Most Holy Place, God has
expended His most special care. Far more is
written of Aaron than of creation, whole chapters
describing what he is to do and what he is not to
do. How beautiful his consecration ; he is first
washed, made perfectly clean, and then anointed.
The anointing was a foreshadowing of Him whose
name is the Messiah, Anointed, the Christ—all
which words set forth the same Divine Person.
Then there was present the bullock for the sin-
offering, also the two rams and the basket of
unleavened bread. These were at the door of the
congregation, whilst the congregation were at the
door of the tent of meeting. What a spectacle
when, arrayed in their appointed garments, Aaron
and his sons—as we might say Christ and His
Church—put their hands on the head of the
bullock, on the sin-offering, and Moses took the
blood and put it on the horns of the altar round
about, satisfying God. Also at the base of the
altar, the very foundation of His Throne, was the
blood brought for His people into God's rest, His
own dwelling-place. Was there ever such a day
in Israel ?

Beautiful is Paul's reference to the Lord as
Priest; he says that under Moses "they indeed have
been made priests many in number," as we have
intimated, because that by death they are hindered

from continuing; but He (Christ), because He "abideth for ever, hath His priesthood unchangeable" (inviolable, R.V.). Elsewhere he speaks of His life as an indissoluble life; unlike the priests that die, "He is able to save to the uttermost" (continually) "them that draw near unto God through Him, seeing He ever liveth to make intercession for them." Oh, my soul, what a Priest! and thy Priest; yea, the Priest of all those who believe—the youngest, the poorest, the weakest, as well as the more advanced or more favoured ones. Hence there is no child of God without his Priest, not a man-made priest, not a priest on earth; One in God's very presence, there ever making intercession for him.

Comforting traits these. He is to offer for our sins, that they lie not on our souls to condemn, and "to give gifts," all in one—*Himself*. To "bear gently with the ignorant and erring." What are we at best but this? Who is He but One who bears gently with us? a bruised reed He will not break; the flax, however feebly burning, He will not quench. What a glass in which to see the love of our only one Priest, who is now in heaven for us, where He never ceases to have us in His mind, to love us, and joy over us when we love Him more, and grieve over us when we doubt or deny Him. It is as if He said, "I come between

you and God; leave your cause with Me; there
is no sin too great for My merit; there is no
need too strong for My grace." He is always
speaking to God of us and for us.

It is when we see Aaron we see what Christ is.

> "A sovereign balm for every wound,
> A cordial for our fear."

How much they lose who do not know what it is.
It is a perpetual occupation on His part for us; He
speaks to God about us, about you and me; had
God a charge (which He has not) Christ would
answer it. Oh, the sweetness of having no guilt
before the eyes of God, no need but He is occupied
in meeting it, no yielding to sin in ourselves over
which He does not grieve, no care He does not
know and provide against, no infirmity of body
or mind with the feeling of which He is not
"touched."

What shall we say of the infinite and ineffable
love, the costliness and the tenderness of which
can be thus ascribed to them? "O thou afflicted,
tossed with tempest, and not comforted, behold, I
will lay thy stones with fair colours, and lay thy
foundations with sapphires."

The very thought of Him thus

> "Makes the wounded spirit whole,
> And calms the troubled breast."

Therefore we repeat, "We have not an High Priest which cannot be touched with the feeling of our infirmities." Thus, what the poor members feel and suffer here is known by Him in heaven : whoever may neglect us, He does not ; whoever may be hardened against us, He is touched by us. What a convergence must there be of all the sorrows and sufferings of His own earth ! And how it tells of His Godhead power, that He knows and can deal with them all ! What a heart so to feel for each one ! Dear, sorrowing, suffering, burdened one, have you a grief ? it touches Him just as a loving mother is touched by the grief, the sorrows, of her child.

How in all this we see the truth of that word, "God, Thy God, hath anointed Thee above Thy fellows. All Thy garments smell of myrrh, and aloes, and cassia"—the sweet ingredients of the anointing oil.

Aaron was first washed—he must be clean who bears the vessels of the Lord—then the oil poured upon him ; then clothed, the white garments for his person, the pure snowy robe for the Holiest, and the garments for glory and for beauty for the Holy Place. All this is seen in our holy great High Priest, pure, perfect in the inner man ; perfect officially before God ; glorious by-and-by when He comes out in His glory—the High Priest for ever after the order of Melchisedec—the King and Priest arrayed in His beauty : bright as the sun, more beautiful than Lebanon, more comely than the cedars.

No marvel Paul should speak of the One whom this represents as greater than all ; He was infinitely greater than Moses, the Lawgiver and King in Jeshurun. Aaron could not compare with Him ; greater than angels, and this He was as *man*. Paul says, " He took not on Him the nature of angels." Another has said, " He left angels where He found them ; they excelled in strength ; they kept not their first estate ; and He left them there." Man excelled in wickedness ; and He came and linked Himself with man, and now we see Him in heaven as our High Priest, ever waiting with reconciliation for sins, and succour for sorrow. The epistle to the Hebrews teems with His divine glories ; it is massive in glory, and ponderous in divine thoughts. And what are we to do ? we are to " consider " Him. But, asks another, what is that ? is it to imitate Him ? The religious mind says so ; but that is not the point of the passage which enjoins it. What business have I to imitate Him in His High Priesthood ? No. I am to " consider " Him as faithful for my sake to God—faithful so that I shall be saved eternally. If I do not consider

Him so, I have blunted the sense of the injunction, and lost the sense of grace. I am to consider Him for my comfort. What a constellation of grace there is in all that! We are to sit *still* before each splendid emblem, and look at Him, and His faithfulness up there, just as we have been considering Aaron.

And let none think they are precluded any of the value of all this, or not entitled to be there; no, all are accepted in the Beloved, all are to call God, Father. There were multitudinous offerers at the altar; but because of the value of the offering, they were all in equal forgiveness and acceptance before God; just as without the offering (without God, as I may say) they were all equally in their sins. To see this would do away with the notion that one man is further off from God than another. Your well-disposed men, as people are pleased to call them, are not a whit nearer to heaven than others, and, though it is a very important matter as far as social interests are concerned, that a man should be a moral rather than an immoral man, yet, let it be clearly understood, that every unsaved man, whatever his walk, is equally far from God; accordingly, as to the unity of the people of God in their standing, they are all equally far from God by nature—all equally ruined and helpless; and when all, by the same act of sovereign distinguishing grace, are brought to believe the gospel of the Lord Jesus Christ, they are equally members of Christ, equally justified, and are all equally righteous before God ; not a shade of difference.

This strikes at the root of all the Pharisaism which is abroad in the world ; one man thinking that he can work himself into a higher standing before God than another.   We maintain as a great truth of Scripture that God Himself in Christ is our Righteousness.   If there be degrees then we cannot understand it ; they have all the same salvation, are saved by the same precious blood, quickened by the same Spirit, and partakers of Christ's death and resurrection.   There is not a shade of difference thus between one and another in the family of God.   As in our spiritual state we are brought into equal fellowship and union with Jehovah, so in our natural state we were in the deadly unity of sin.

> " Oh, the welcome I have found there !
>   God in all His love made known !
> Oh, the glory that surrounds there !
>   Those accepted in His Son.
> Who can tell the depths of bliss
> Spoken by the Father's kiss ? "

And whilst in the sweets of that kiss, how glorious to dwell on the finished and the unfinished

work which Christ undertook.   Atonement for sin
is finished when He cried that one word "finished."
Heaven and earth, hell and death, the grave and
corruption, all heard the wondrous word of triumph,
all stood in an altered position.   But the *unfinished*
—His intercession for us is not finished, His supply
of pardons for us is not finished, His communica-
tions with His Father respecting us are not finished ;
His comforts and consolations, the performance of
His promises, are not finished ; the "I will never
leave thee" promises, when passing through the
fire and the waters, they are not finished ; the
power which verifies the promise that no man can
pluck us out of His hands is not finished ; and
in a glorious sense His lovely ministries for our
joy and our rejoicing will go on for ever and ever.
There may be an end of all else, but never of His
love or of His grace ; like Himself, these are
eternal and unchanging.

Oh, vast, fathomless abyss of grace and mercy,
that God should lift man out of his sin and misery,
leading on to an interminable hell, and place him
on so high a height !   And unfathomable grace
and love is it in Christ, who is what He now is for
us in the presence of God.

Through the one, that is, God's love and grace,
we have been reconciled by the death of Christ,
and through the other we are saved by His life.

The High Priest of Israel in His Robes
of Glory and Beauty

11

The Holy Garments

"And thou shalt make holy garments for Aaron thy brother, for glory and for beauty...that he may minister unto Me in the priest's office. And these are the garments which they shall make; a breastplate, and an ephod, and a robe, and a broidered coat, a mitre, and a girdle."—Exodus 28:2-4

WE have now to see the High Priest in his robes. The word "robes" often appears in Scripture. In sublime figure the Divine Being is described as "clothed with light as with a garment." Christ on the holy mount was "clothed in raiment white and glistening." The palm-bearing multitudes were "clothed with white robes;" the king's daughter has "clothing of wrought gold;" and Sardis is to "walk with Me," said the Lord, "in white." On these Tabernacle robes the eye may rest with delight, how rich the pen that could describe them! How much I myself owe, through a life now nearing its close, to the moment when first my eyes were directed to Aaron and his glories and all this Tabernacle truth; it became central, diffusing itself through the whole revelation of God.

Dr. Watts has exhorted—

"Sing the *full* glories of the Lamb."

And here they are; for it is in God's own appointed priest, when robed in his magnificent attire, that we see these glories, whether in his present, relative, or official glory; whether with the unsullied robe of white he performs his work of love in the Holiest, or has on his magnificent garments, with the names of Israel bound in brightness to his person; it is all grand to contemplate.   As he stood in his robes he was simply beautiful — Christ's glorious Person and our glory as connected with Him all shining out in this typical man.   It is not a place which we have to consider so much as a person.   The gold, the blue, scarlet, purple, and fine-twined linen; the golden chains, the precious stones, with all their variegated hues and deep engravings; the mitre crown of gold and lace of blue; and all the beauteous veil-work, curtain-work, altars of gold, and penetrating the Holiest—marvels excelling all, indicating what He is.   Could aught be added to make it all more costly or more beautiful?

The whole presents a profusion of interest, each

part containing some type of the unsearchable riches which are lodged in Christ for us. How much they lose who fail to read, or if reading fail to perceive, the things that God has laid up for them that love Him! Over how many a lovely landscape the eye of the stolid and ignorant roams thoughtlessly and ignorantly. May we not all pray, "Open Thou mine eyes that I may behold wondrous things out of Thy law." There is not a colour here, not a thread of tapestry, not a lineament of beauty as in the faces of the cherubim, not a sparkle of the real manifested glory, not a sound of golden bells, which have not a depth of meaning as much, and one might say even more, than that which occupied the Divine mind when He filled this shoreless universe with all its varied resplendent worlds of light, and the unnumbered creatures of His power. It is neither grammar nor Greek, nor a question of learning, nor of deep study, but of the eyes of the understanding being opened. Hence the sweet annals of many of the poor who live and die richly, knowing the only true God and Jesus Christ whom He hath sent.

The garments are called "Holy Garments," and also "garments for glory and for beauty," which they could not have been had they not been holy, for without holiness there could be no glory, no beauty. Holiness lies at the foundation of the divine character ; without it God could not be what He is : holiness and innocence are different ; innocence is where there is no knowledge of evil as at first in the garden, but holiness is compatible with a knowledge of, but separation from, evil.

Shall we first look at

THE WHITE ROBES?

There was the white inner robe described in Exodus xxviii., which extended from the loins downwards. The embroidered coat of fine linen was a pure white robe, proper to the person of Aaron, and had the aspect of damask ; there was also a white girdle of the same. Once in the year Aaron wore his long, simple, ample robe of entire white flowing down to his feet ; a white linen girdle bound it to his person. In Aaron's hands is a vessel with the blood of the newly-slain victim ; some few drops of it are on his robe, some on the mercy-seat, and some on the ground where he stood ; for the earth needed to be purged of its curse. It was in the Most Holy Place that Aaron in this robe performed that which has been called "the top height of his priesthood." Other priests simply served ; they killed and offered sacrifices, but none save the high priest could approach the Holy of Holies which *he* did, but not without blood ; that was essential.

If we want an image of Christ, as He now is, we have it here. The white array and the sprinkled blood are the two things most prominent: the white garment shows His intrinsic perfectness, the blood the character of His work. It was this, with his eye fully set upon Christ, that led Paul to say, " I know *whom* I have believed," and " I am ready to be offered."

On this Luther says—

> " If faith His blood strikes on the door,
>   Death can never harm us more."

Oh, it is Christ thus pourtrayed who is the true object for the heart! The blood is for the conscience.

This embroidered coat was Aaron's innermost garment, put on after the washing with water: it was all of linen. There where no mortal eye could pierce, all was perfect. In heart and thought, in will and desire, the Lord was intrinsically perfect. The searching glance of divine holiness could detect no spot or stain of sin in Him; He was unsullied, He was pure, He was essentially and absolutely perfect.

How vital is our own interest in this divine perfectness! when we are "black, but comely;" "vile," said Job, "unclean," said Isaiah; "filthy," said God, concerning Joshua: it was when all

these (who are true exponents of what we are)
saw God, they saw themselves. Thus was it with
our first parents; the moment they knew sin
they would fain fly and hide themselves from
God's sight. What a change! they abhorred
themselves. But God in mercy provided *the first
clothing*, hiding from His eye and from their own
view, their nakedness; they tried to cover themselves, but could not do it; God did it by death.
The devil's provision consisted of fig leaves, image
of our own doings, religious performances, bodily
afflictions, self-mortification, ordinances, prayers,
gifts, penances. With us who are in Christ (so
is the Pauline doctrine) it is not so much that
we are clothed by Christ, *we are as Christ.* Our
old Adam selves are never covered up, but condemned. Wonderful when we are awakened to
see this; our own vileness of nature and sins
all put away from before God; wonderful too,
then, our sense of sin! In the words of another,
" My sins are so numerous and aggravated that
I am ashamed to recognize them as mine, and
am tempted to relieve myself by another sin—
that of disowning and denying myself, as though
I could discover another self less guilty. O God,
to Thee who alone art my God, my devotion
was a falsehood and a lie: I called upon Thee,
but I fled from Thee; I said Thou wert my God,

but I lied. Woe were me if angels had to judge
me; if I had to judge myself, my lot were
wretched and disastrous. Hence my knowing
Thee, blessed Lord, has prevailed more with me
than that knowledge of myself which would lead
me not to dare to present myself before Thee."

Christ now appears as our great High Priest
with this spotless robe, having special offices of
love and grace for us. He is there as in John xiii.,
and He is there as in 1 John ii. 1, to give God an
answer to everything He has to see or say concerning us. God's children are thus in the value of
this white robe ; in themselves the most pure have
some shade of evil, like the dead fly in the pot of
ointment ; but in Christ all excellencies dwell
with not a shadow or a shade to mar them. Sweet,
personal likeness to Christ will heaven bring.
"*Arrayed in white robes*" is what is ascribed to us ;
to remain white, spotless for ever, will be the
wonderful thing ; it will well befit the inheritance
which is incorruptible, undefiled, and will never
fade away. Splendour and purity beautifully
combine, both personal and both absolute, pure,
perfect for ever.

> " Not a stain, a new creation,
>   Ours is such a full salvation."

The white robe was bound to Aaron's person by

THE GIRDLE OF NEEDLEWORK.

This speaks of *service;* and the Lord is often in the Word shown to us as being girded : He was by special emphasis "the Servant." He Himself said, "I delight to do Thy will, O My God ; yea, Thy law is within My heart." His whole life was one of service, hence we see Him girded with the girdle—the emblem of service.

When He washed the disciples' feet He took a towel and *girded* Himself ; and when He comes in glory He will *gird* Himself, and come forth and serve us. For those whom He finds *watching* will He gird Himself, and make them to sit down to meat, and come forth and serve them. To those who love His appearing He will give a crown, to those occupying for Him He will give cities. Thus, for those *watching*, He will not only gird Himself, but will make them to sit down to meat, and will come forth and serve them : the *watchers* get the best. Love delights in serving. Service is love's sweetest enjoyment, there is something beautiful in this posture of girding.

Do you ask *where* He wears this girdle ? Here in type we have Him wearing the girdle round *His loins*. This He did that in fullest power and strength He may be always ready for service for us. Thus it was He girded Himself for His work down here; and thus it is He wears His girdle *now*. But when He comes forth for judgment by-and-by He will be girt about the paps with a *golden* girdle. Oh, think of Him as girded about the heart, the seat of His affections! as much as to say, " I must gird up My loins surely for My own; My girdle must not be loose; but all My *love* especially must be girt up for My saints in the day when the thunders of judgment let loose for destruction are rolling on every side." Oh, what comfort for His weak, trembling Israel, who will be saying, " How will it be with us in the day of His threatened vengeance?" Ah! He will have a special office to perform for His own in that day. He knows they will need His services in the moment of overwhelming indignation; therefore He will be girt about *His heart*, the seat of His divine, unchangeable affections.

We have said the Lord was a Servant; but how did He serve? What was the principle of all His service? Its blessedness consisted in His doing the will of His Father; in having no will apart from Him. Our blessedness consists in simply and only doing the same. When the Lord had to do anything, it was with this thought He girded Himself—this is for My Father's glory; and we also are to be girded about the loins with this principle of doing *all for Him*. And blessed

is that servant whom the Lord when He cometh
shall find so doing.

But now besides the white robe we have

THE ROBE OF BLUE,

or the robe of the ephod. The blue occupies a
large place in the Tabernacle, and especially on
the person of Aaron; he wore the robe of blue
magnificently woven, reaching near to his feet.
Appended are golden bells of melodious sound,
and golden fruit; image of the pomegranate which
was beautiful in appearance, and of fragrant odour.
The inner robe, just described, was snow white,
and visible only at the feet; though unseen it
was carefully and elaborately made; this in
lovely contrast is blue. This robe was called
the robe of beauty; also the robe of odours, and
this latter because the oil of delicious fragrance
poured on the head of Aaron ran down his whole
person, mingling with the precious stones on his
breast, and extending down to the very hem of
his garments. This robe was for service in the
Holy Place; nothing wanting, it reached down
from the head to the feet. The softness of its
colour made it so beautiful—blue has always
been the colour of beauty; we think how from
childhood we always liked it, as one writes—

"... the linked sky and sea with the one blue
That maketh both so passing beautiful."

And another—

"The glorious blue serene, mirrored by the ocean's depths."

Do we not get up to our fullest height in our conceptions of Christ, when we contemplate Him as intrinsically and eternally *heavenly*. What beauty of essence! what beauty of character! No angel could depict Him. We read that Christ and His members are all of one—of one sort. Sweetly the blue (the heavenly, the holy, the gracious) mingles itself in all that He is in Himself towards us, and in all that we are as one with Him. Our heavenliness dates (if date it ever had) in the mind of God ever since God was God, from all eternity. "Chosen in Him before the foundation of the world." We are blessed, in the divine purpose, "with all spiritual blessings, in heavenly places in Christ Jesus." And "as we have borne the image of the earthy," poor, sinful, sorrowing, dying ones, "we shall also bear the image of the heavenly," the holy, glorious, and majestic One. When God acts upon us here it is from heaven. "Except a man be born again [or *from above*] he cannot enter into the kingdom of heaven." It is in heaven now we have our citizenship; it is its politics, and not those of earth, that regulate our actions and our life. We take our cue from heaven, and not from the government or rulers of earth, as to what shall be or shall not be in this world. John the apostle tells us that as He is, so are we.

And here I should like to draw out a little that word in 1 Corinthians i. 9. As we look up into heaven at the High Priest there it is sweet to think of it—"God is faithful, by whom ye were called unto the fellowship of His Son Jesus Christ our Lord." It is God who hath called us. He was the beginning of the old creation ; He created all things by the word of His power. And He is the beginning of the new creation : only this, that which is first recorded in the Word is modern compared with His purpose concerning us. That to which we are called is participation with Christ, or, as here said, "*the fellowship of His Son Jesus Christ.*" Fellowship, communion, and participation are interchangeable words, showing the same thing. How wonderful ! called to a participation of all that Christ is and has, or that could be communicated. What creature in his own standing as such could sit upon the throne with Christ, or be joint-heir with Him of His eternal possessions ? it goes beyond all thought of man or angel. Communion means share and share alike—participation the same. But of what ? We read in Titus i. of "eternal life, which God, that cannot

lie, promised before the world began;" that is,
before creation had a beginning; promised, not
to us, not having then existence, but to Christ;
promised in covenant on the ground that Christ
would do God's will in dying, so saving man, and
doing justice to God's law and character in saving
him.   Hence the certainty of eternal life.   "I give
unto them eternal life, and they shall never
perish, neither shall any man pluck them out of
My hand."   We read too of Christ's image, we
are to participate in His form, His likeness, "predestinated to be conformed to the image of His
Son;" and in His heavenly endowments, because
we are sons, He hath sent forth the Spirit of His
Son, "whereby we cry, Abba Father."   And
also in His possessions we participate.   "The
Father loveth the Son, and hath given all things
into His hand," so that all things are His; and
now He says, "The glory which Thou gavest
Me I have given them."   All things, all worlds,
angels, dominions, principalities, and powers all
ours; we possess them with Christ; all this is
truly heavenly.

But it was here on earth the foundation for all
was laid in death, a death accepted by God who
raised Christ from the dead.   We have died in His
death, and are alive in His life, and are now in the
same hope of glory and destined to the same home.

All this tells of the character of our calling—it is heavenly. The timeless, ineffable share assigned to us by God in the future course of Him who is Head of the Church, which is His body, being of His flesh and His bones. The certainty of it is that God is faithful by whom we are thus called. Could we be more associated with the Son of God or with heaven? could our hope be greater? No marvel that with such connection with the heavenly Christ Himself could say, "the Son of Man, which is in heaven," thus linking man with heaven, giving us, in and through Him, a place there, and all made sure.

Poor Christianity which has become what it is in the present day, how few ever ask the question, "Is my life in keeping with all this? or is my knowledge even in keeping with it?" Since such a life as Paul the apostle and John the beloved how has the crown fallen, and the fine gold become dim! Is the Church as we see it any more than the poor world growing better? And as scepticism rather than truth seems to prevail, how are we reminded of the words, "When the Son of man cometh, shall He find faith on the earth?"

What thoughts upon thoughts meet us here, calculated to awaken the conscience and to benefit our lives!

In this heavenly robe provision was made that

"there shall be a hole in the top of it, in the midst thereof; it shall have a binding of woven work round about the hole of it, as it were the hole of a habergeon, *that it be not rent.*" Thus the binding was strong as a breastplate of armour; none could rend it. That which Christ wears for Himself and for us is never to be rent—unchangeable, secure are we in His deep love. No condemnation, no separation. Was there heavenliness in the blue and purity in the embroidered coat all of white, and in the inner garb for the person of Aaron? there is security, there is glory in this.

The word "*pluck*" is a most significant one. "No one," saith the Lord, "shall pluck them out of My hand." It shows what awful forces are against us: enemies inborn and hell-born, especially the adversary, the devil, walking about seeking whom he may devour. But their labour is in vain. He says *no one*, "No one" (R.V.) "shall pluck them out of My hand."

Another word is sweetly significant; it is the word "*keep.*" What a fountain of consolation to the fearful, or the weary, or the one lying at the gate of death is that promise, "Behold, I am with thee, and will keep thee!" It is not, "I will help thee;" that is much, but, "I will keep thee." Can words of sweeter security fill the heart in living or in dying—"He will keep"?

Moreover, this garment was all of one piece, all of equal texture. There may be as men see us, and there is, division and sad inequality of life and walk, many oppositions of belief, spots and blemishes that Paul could speak of only with weeping. Yet it is not so, as God sees us in His Son; not only no spot or blemish, but no inequalities like the fine flour of the meat-offering sacrifice, each grain uniform and perfect, bought by the same blood, therefore of equal value; indwelt by the same spirit, blest by the same place before God, arranged, settled by God before the foundation of the world.

Wonderful as a piece of work is

THE EPHOD.

It was laden with all glorious things. He had fitted, as it were, to Himself all that He needed for the work He had to do. Of it Josephus writes: "The ephod in figure, similar to an ordinary coverlet fastened by two golden clasps, in which were set two large and beautiful sardonyx, bearing the names of those from whom the tribes were denominated." Its texture, made of gold, is interwoven with scarlet, purple, and fine-twined linen. On the front, attached to it, and never to be loosened from it, is the breast-plate inlaid with twelve precious stones, all varied in colour and beauty, with the names of the children of Israel engraven on them.

We must not omit

THE CURIOUS GIRDLE.

We see it all around the high priest's person ; this was not a girdle for strength, but simply for binding the ephod to the person.

"The expression, 'The curious girdle,'" Mr. Soltau remarks, "literally is according to the old writers, and *ephodized* him with it, the object apparently being to convey the thought that this curious belt so connected the ephod with the person who wore it, as to impart to him all the virtues it contained ;" namely, the preciousness of the gold, the perfectness, heavenliness, and all the other qualities intended by the blue and the scarlet and the fine-twined linen.

But now lovely variety, for we cannot longer tarry here. Casting your eyes downwards at the hems of this robe, we see the

BELLS OF GOLD.

Sweet those bells ! One seems to hear their gentle sound. Luther remarks on music—and it may be appropriated here—" Music is the only art of the prophets that can calm the agitation of the soul ;" adding, "It is one of the most delightful presents God has given us." The sound of these bells was dependent on the movements of the high priest as he went to and fro in his service.

"It shall be upon Aaron to minister: and his sound shall be heard when he goeth in unto the holy place before the Lord, and when he cometh out." That is, as I understand, only such sounds as are according to God, could be allowed to come from the world into His presence; and only such sounds could go forth *from* the divine presence to the world. What a lesson for us, who professedly so often go in and out before the Lord, that we indulge not in any of earth's confused and confusing sounds! We know how one person, entering any sacred scene or home circle of piety, may bring only the world with him, and leaving take nothing of the atmosphere in which he has been. How these holy bells told Aaron's movements now at the golden altar—now going in, and now coming out! Our High Priest has gone in, and the sound of *Him we have heard*. The Spirit came down at Pentecost and told of His being there. It is the same Spirit within us that alone can tell

"How sweet the name of Jesus sounds!"

Thus all around the lower part of the robe were these bells and

THE ODORIFEROUS POMEGRANATES

in succession. How rich truly, and how lovely—all in bright and beauteous colours! for the bells were gold, and the pomegranates blue, purple, and red. We read in Solomon's Song that the bridegroom's temples are represented as the pomegranate shining forth behind his locks as objects of special loveliness and admiration, and that when he went out to the garden the very budding of them was attractive to him ; and now here they are all plentiful, suspended along with the bells of gold, on this beauteous robe of blue.

"Were the bells off," as another has suggested, "the garment would be silent." Separated from Christ, we have no joy, can give no testimony, can bear no fruit. Moreover, as again suggested, "it is just as we follow Him within the veil, and are subject to every motion of the head, the shoulders, and the heart of our High Priest, that we bear our proper witness for the living though hidden Christ." But the pomegranate tells of fruit, and if we are in communion with our Head, there will flow down the rich fruit, as there will be rich harmony—sweet music of testimony, joy, and praise in our life. And whilst the garment was extending far up the person of the high priest, these bells and pomegranates hung near to the ground. Though our Head is above, His members are to manifest the fruit, and bear the testimony down here ; not fruit only, but joy, for the bells may indicate joy also—joy in the midst of our testimony. But the fruitfulness and the joy will be alike in connection *with Him*, and must flow *from Him*. The bells were of gold—divine joy; precious in its nature, and costly in its value. He, the Divine One, who bought us with such a price, is the spring of all joy, the source of all fruitfulness; we "rejoice with joy unspeakable and full of glory." He who weighed the mountains in His scales, and measured every starry orb, had from everlasting weighed the value and sweetness of this lovely growth of fruit, and the place it would occupy in setting forth His own beauty and preciousness.

Proverbial is the pomegranate in its own suited clime for the value and beauty of its fruit, and the sweetness of its odours, yet is it the fruit of earthly soil. Christ is in heaven, but the fruit following from His death is from below, and is seen here below, work of His own Spirit in us through the blessed Word. Thus in every saved soul Christ gathers fruit for Himself from out of this sin-stricken wilderness world. And by-and-by we shall see Him our High Priest, in the day of the glory, laden with the joy of heaven, and the fruit of the once sin-cursed earth. Can we not say as He did, "He that cometh from heaven is above all: He beareth witness of what He hath seen and heard: *He is above all*"?

We now turn to

THE HOLY ANOINTING OIL.

It is God again who names the ingredients; His thought is a perfect odour. He who had formed nature knew whence to extract the essences to set forth what was infinitely precious.

Their several names remind us of their value. *Myrrh* signifies the soother of pain, which truly Christ is, a soother of the sufferings and sorrows of all His own, in life, and in death the same; by His Spirit through His Word, He does this. The family of Bethany, the little circle at Nain, the house of Jairus, are witnesses of how He soothed and rejoiced bereaved hearts. It was the sight the proto-martyr Stephen had of Him, in the hour of his martyrdom, which lifted him above the fear and sense of death. Sin brings pain and remorse which eat up the flesh, causing man's beauty to "consume away like a moth;" myrrh, that drops from the bleeding bark, may remind us of the flow of His blood on the tree which assuages the griefs of the sin-sick soul. And as to the backsliding soul when the bride in the Song had lost her communion, and was sore distressed, He left on the latch of her door which had been closed against Him, a portion of "sweet-smelling myrrh," that on opening, her fingers dropping with the odours, may remind her of Him—the tenderness and preciousness of His love unchanging, though *she* had changed.

Another of the ingredients is *Cassia*, an outer bark sweet and fragrant; another, *Sweet Cinnamon*, an inner bark sweet and fragrant; and *Calamus*, which is the pith, sweet and fragrant. These all were pure primeval spices to make an oil of holy ointment—an ointment compound after the art of the apothecary — that apothecary being instructed by God Himself. How perfect was it! the type in itself was perfect, and its design. What did it typify but that of which the beloved disciple, St. John the aged, wrote when he said, "ye have an unction from the Holy One, and ye know all things." That Christ Himself received the anointing, we read, "Thy God hath anointed Thee with the oil of gladness above Thy fellows. All Thy garments smell of myrrh, and aloes, and cassia, out of the ivory palaces, whereby they have made Thee glad;" and as we can never separate the Church from Christ, if we are but a thread even of those garments, we are in the value of His anointing. Upon Aaron, who typified the Lord, it was poured, it was not *poured* on others, but the oil was poured upon *his* head. "The precious ointment upon the head, that ran down upon the beard, even Aaron's beard: that

went down to the skirts of his garments." Not
a thread but was sweet with the odours of it; the
humblest or youngest as much as the greatest
in the school of Christ is in one anointing.

These odours tell of Christ's preciousness,
especially the delights of His Person. How
something exquisite through this anointing is
the delight which Christ and His redeemed have
in each other! The words of the bride are sweet
echoes, answering and re-answering to some well-
loved sounds of the Bridegroom's voice; hear
what He says, "How fair is thy love, my sister,
my spouse; how much better is thy love than
wine, and the smell of thine ointments than all
spices. The smell of thy garments is like the
smell of Lebanon; thy garden [a paradise of fruits
and odours] is my sister, my spouse.* But the
odours so grateful thus are *His* odours, as the
blessed Spirit and heavenly graces are *His* graces,
and *His* Spirit, and are *His* bestowments upon us.
The Beloved according to her is as gold. His
head is as fine gold; "the chiefest" (the most
conspicuous and signalized) "among ten thousand;
yea, He is altogether lovely." She is as Tirzah
to Him, which means *pleasantness*. "Thou art
beautiful, oh, my love, as pleasantness." He says
the daughters saw her, and blessed her (that is,

* *English Woman's Bible.*

pronounced her happy); yea, the queen and the
concubines, and they praised her!

In leaving all for Him, the daughter would
forget her own people and her father's house;
He having on His part, "greatly desired her
beauty." Rebekah leaving all for Isaac, and
Rachael going with Jacob whom she loved and
who was the loved of Jacob, were sweet fore-
shadowings of Him thus. * Happy for every
believer to know he is in all these loves. The
oil ran down from Aaron's head to the hem of his
garment; the oil of gladness, telling of what was
infinitely more precious than itself: it was typical
of the blessed Spirit which as in all fulness the oil
was poured on Aaron, so without measure was it
given to Him. Typical, too, was the oil of the
setting apart of those who received it, as David
was anointed to the throne, and the blessed Lord
for His great work. "Anointed," Messiah, Christ,
are one word and have one and the same meaning.
"Holy" shows how He is set apart, and we in
Him free from evil, separate from all that defileth,
and freed from all that condemneth.

Surely it is solemn to note that nothing did
God admit to service that was not anointed.
The brazen altar, the golden altar, the mercy
seat, and indeed all the vessels were anointed.

* See *Brides of Scripture.*

Let us think, God owns no service which is not possessed of His own unction. Alas! to how many will He say, "*I* never knew you;" the world knew you; the Church knew you; but *I* never knew you. It is a great subject, and wonderful for a believer to say, "I have in me the same One that from all eternity was in Christ, the One who knew the Father and the Son, as none other ever knew." Because we are sons, He hath sent forth the Spirit of the Son (the same Spirit that was and is in Him); whereby we say, as He from all eternity has done, " Abba, Father."

Corresponding with the Ephod, made after its work, gold, blue, purple, scarlet, and fine twined linen, is

THE BREASTPLATE.

What a vision the tribes enjoyed when Aaron came out in his robes for glory and for beauty— their own names recorded on his breast and on his arm. Deep engravenment!

> "Where nor time nor age could ever cause
> Them wasting or decay."

Kings and princes have had their names erased or changed, but no name once recorded as belonging to Christ can ever be changed. No; this breastplate could not fall below the heart, for the golden chains held it up; nor rise above, for the loops of blue held it down.   On this breast-plate were the most exquisite

PRECIOUS STONES.

To the ordinary eye, these are simply beauteous things of art; but to the opened understanding they are full of Christ, the varied coloured precious stones forming a glory, broken up into distinctive exquisite hues, answering to the holy loveliness of the redeemed. These had a perfection in them-selves beyond all compare. But it is the moral— the application of it all to Christ and His re-deemed, that makes everything of such deep unending interest.

Upon the shoulders of the ephod there are two onyx stones, and upon the breastplate are other stones. Remark a very important difference between them : the onyx stones upon the shoulder were of one colour—there was no difference; but among the stones upon the breast no two were alike. There was emerald, there was blue, there was red, and every gorgeous colour, all in beautiful variety. But on the shoulder there were the two onyx stones of one and the same colour. There is an all-likeness and yet a wondrous variedness in all who are redeemed. And now more particularly as to these onyx stones. Where do we find the onyx stone first? the earliest mention of it is in

Genesis ii., the next is here in Exodus, then again
we find it in Ezekiel, and lastly in the Revelation.
We first see it amid the unfallen glories of Eden,
but with no names engraven on it there—no
inscription there—as if to show that the mark of
property, of true, eternal ownership, could not be
affixed to these stones, until the price, so to speak,
had been paid. But where do we next meet with
them? Upon the shoulders of the high priest,
shining there—yea, brightly—bearing the names
of Israel's tribes. Thus, in virtue of His redeeming blood, our High Priest has raised these stones
from earth to Himself, and has engraven upon
them names which associate them with all the
dignity and glory of His own Person. See these
stones, both of one colour, shining resplendently
on Aaron's shoulders. Thus Christ bears His
redeemed upon His shoulders, all His saints are
upheld by His strength, and all in relation to
each other, and to Him all are one family, have
one faith, one blessed and glorious salvation, one
God, one heaven.

This is the onyx stone truth; the oneness, the
all-likeness of believers. On the shoulders, simi-
larity; on the breastplate, variety—there, no two
of these brilliants are the same. I have not your
gifts, nor have you the responsibilities which are
mine. Your calling as to service is not mine, nor

is mine yours. Paul was not John, nor was John Paul; each had his own special measure of grace, and each *his own gift*. One labourer need not envy another. When we get into the coming glory how shall we marvel that here we ever looked coldly on one whom God was using more than another! The onyx stones were all engraven according to *birth*, those on the breastplate according to *tribes*. Very beautiful they look all set in gold, and worn before the Lord continually, so that He could not look upon Aaron without seeing them! How suffused were they with the pure light of the sanctuary—those golden lamps of sevenfold brightness! Do we live in this sweet thought? Our God cannot look upon the heart of Christ without seeing you and me. Wondrous mystery! depths and heights are there untraceable and unfathomable in such grace and love. Let me ask, Do you know your place thus upon His heart continually? "A name of joy—may we just rest in the sweetness of it, and look up and realize how intensely the Lord joys over us."

> " My God, why dost Thou love me so?
>   What hast Thou seen in me
> To make my happiness so great,
>   So dear a joy to Thee?"

How blessed when He is able to say of us, " How fair and how pleasant art thou, O love, for delights." Then, too, we must not forget the corresponding blessedness of having *Him* on our heart continually.

Precious thought! the Father's eye cannot rest upon His Son in response to His Son's ineffable delight, but it must drop upon these stones—must gaze on each one. Ah! do we see it? There we are, your place and mine, down upon the breast —the seat of the affections, and on the shoulders the place of strength. And these stones were embedded in gold, all set, shall I say it? in divine casings. Not only are we *in* God, but we are held *by* God. Happy theme! for I might go on and on about the stones, and the names, and the wreathen chains, and ouches, all indicating the position of unity and safety and acceptance of every child of God in association with the risen Lord; so that in the presence of God each one is there in a divine right; for the Lord brings us in along with Himself, giving us the same title to that Presence which He Himself possesses.

But further, each stone, as I have said, had on it a *name.* There was no name on the stones in Eden; but after atonement had been made we find these stones bearing God-given names; and though Israel for the present may seem to be lost, the stones have revival in Ezekiel, and are in the *New Jerusalem.* No stone bearing the divine inscription can be finally lost. And as with Israel, so with *us ;* no child of God can perish. "My sheep," Jesus Himself said of His own, "shall never perish, neither shall any man pluck them out of My hand." The precious stones themselves were, as we have seen, beauteous, endurable, with no seeds of decay in them. Their adorning consists of the names which Jewish writers tell us were in raised letters, "adding richer shades, and making brilliancy more brilliant, and loveliness more lovely." Suggestively how we are reminded of the brilliancy of the redeemed, and the glory of the moment when the corruptible shall have put on incorruption, and the mortal immortality. Gold in these scenes always speaks to us of the divine, we are brought by the gospel to Christ, and by Christ to *God.* Why did He die ? Was it merely to pluck us from an abyss of an endless woe ? was it only to save us from hell ? No ; but to bring us to God, beyond which eternally nothing can be greater. These precious stones are for a remembrancer. It is said of Zion, "I have graven thee upon the palms of My hands." Lord, the simile is sweet, but no simile of Thee is enough—no fancy of the mind, no sweetest dream. Yet even the dream may be sweet. Escaping from a wreck, losing all but her two fatherless little ones, a young widow in her

grief sank into a deep sleep, burying her sorrows,
thinking only of her Saviour, when lo! like one of
the visions of the olden time, the Lord stood
present to her view, His face filled with greatest
tenderness. To assure her of her place in His love,
He showed her His hand white as parian marble,
then lifting it up, He displayed her own name
graven upon it, saying, "I have graven thee upon
the palms of My hands." Such a sight was it that
ever after all her sorrows and all her losses were as
nothing; she never lost the joy of it, so remindful
of His word, so assuring of His love, until she
passed beyond the storms and shadows that had
overtaken her, to where—

> "Not a wave of trouble rolls
> Across the peaceful breast."

But another thing, the stones were *linked together*,
linked in lovely chains of gold; little golden clasps
bound them to each other and to Aaron; none
could get away or part with the rest. We cannot
be separated from Christ, nor from each other. It
is all aside from the truth to talk of a really
separated, divided church; there is no such thing.
The church as God sees it is one, and no power of
hell can ever separate that church from its risen
Head in heaven; we are bound up together in the
one eternal counsel, in the one electing love. Oh,
none need cherish envy or feelings of animosity

against another! For aught I know, I may be bound by one of these lovely links to the very one whom I am treating with indifference or dislike, or against whom I am cherishing an unloving spirit. Gaze on this robe; practically and sinfully Judah may vex Ephraim, and Ephraim Judah; but in the sight of God they are side by side in the breastplate and on the shoulders; they could not help themselves.

We have observed how the onyx stones were in Eden. It is interesting, according to the meaning of the name, which signifies "the breaking forth of glory," to trace these stones, now for a while appearing, and then for a time apparently lost, and then by-and-by re-appearing in revived and enhanced beauty, God getting, so to speak, His own revival of His own ways and purposes of love. For after that sin had come in by the fall, and had thrown its deep shadow over Eden and Eden's glory, destroying or dimming the brightness of these stones, how blessed to see them reviving again as here in Exodus! Then, after gleaming with resplendent lustre upon the Aaronic shoulder, and after complete failure had impressed its stamp upon the Mosaic economy, and the kingly rule which succeeded it, how happy to meet with them again, revived and beautiful amid the fair glory of the millennial age! And then after the millennium, and after the terrible wrath, in the midst of which the earth and the heavens will be dissolved by fire, there will emerge the new heavens and the new earth, in the which these stones will shine again amid the four-square city of the new Jerusalem, the scene of their final glory, the place of their eternal establishment.

How singular is it to see the puzzle resting on the minds of the greatest scientists of the day as to any such time to come! Some dream about a golden age; but how it will come, by what means, they know not. One writing for the rest says, "It is hard to resist the conclusion that the golden year is after all a will-o'-the-wisp, which is to draw us onward, but remain inaccessible,

> "'Whose margin fades
> For ever and for ever when I move.'"

Great are the uncertainties of minds dark towards God, and His revealed purposes which through all the ages are the same! They never can define what the future of man or time will be. If their "grand era" is coming, when will it be here? and how will it come? Some tell of progress, but progress is what is merely to transpire on earth. No; that which will bring an age of golden brightness and blessedness to this long-suffering world and groaning creation is not of man or by man, neither by his works, or by so-called progress, but

by the glorious appearing on this earth of a veritable Person or BEING who only hath light and
immortality, King of kings, and Lord of lords.
Men dream of ages; God speaks of "*one day*."
They hope in progress; God wants nothing of
man's help or man's mending—poor help and
miserable mending will it be ; for when the Coming
One shall have come will He find faith on the
earth ? No; our God shall come, and all His saints
with Him.   Men ironically say the time they look
for, they suppose, "will drop from the skies." True,
indeed, but not in the way they frivolously imagine.

And now, in conclusion, what are we doing with
ourselves—with God's jewels ?   Where and how
are we living ?   Are we here—here consciously on
the Lord's bosom, resting in His affections ? With
such a place, what manner of persons ought we to
be as believers ?   If we do not know what we are,
or what we have, we shall probably go on with
self and with the world ; but if we know ourselves
to be heirs of God, joint-heirs with Christ, where
or what will our place be here ?   Oh, let us not
name the name of Christ on our lips if we bear
not the impress of Christ in our lives ! It is the
holy knowledge of position that gives the highest
life, we *are* His jewels—to Him so costly, so
precious, that He bought us with His own blood ;
and are we to use ourselves as we please ? Oh,

no, no! we are not our own to use. Just imagine ourselves down on His heart, and then our life going out in some act of wrong. Just imagine ourselves yonder, in the Person of our living Head, in calm acceptance there—"inside the veil"—and yet our spirits down here in levity and worldliness and forgetfulness of God. This jewel truth touches us under all circumstances—in our ways and in our words, and in all that we do. A jewel of heaven is not to be used and abused by Satan as if it were his property; we are the property of Christ, the purchase of the precious blood of Christ.

In connection with the breastplate are

THE URIM AND THUMMIM

which Israel consulted in all times of need, and in all cases of perplexity. They were put *in* the breastplate, not *on* it, as were the precious stones, but folded in it. These lovely appendages are all held together by, and suspended on, the curious girdle of the ephod by chains of gold above, and a lace of blue below, which fastened the breastplate to the ephod. We are not told what they were, we do not know how they imparted the needed guidance, but there they were in seeming mystery, lodged for Israel in the high-priestly robe. We know that Urim and Thummim, as to the words, signify "light and perfection,"

beautifully comprising all that the sinner or God
can require. "Light" claimed all from Israel
that God could possibly require, and "perfection"
showed that God on His part had found in Himself all that Israel could need.

The stones were set about this light and
perfection of God, just as all the redeemed are
around God—God the centre of all ; so here we
have these lines of stones placed in order, like the
arrangement of the tents surrounding the Tabernacle—God in the midst of all.

But then, as to the guiding or leading which
God gave to Israel through the mysterious way,
we have something, may I not say ? far beyond
it.   In Psalm xxxii. God says, " I will guide thee
with Mine eye."   We have no need now, as Israel
of old, to resort, in order to know God's mind (as
with the mystic Urim and Thummim) to any one
particular spot.   He never leaves, but ever follows
His child, who has but to look up and watch His
eye.   Oh, ye perplexed and troubled ones, now
out on the lonely desert, threading the intricacies
of the wilderness path, often dark, often mazy,
have you come to a point in the journey where
two paths present themselves for your choice ?
You have only to look upwards to your Father's
eye ; and as that eye alights upon your path, and
sheds its radiance upon the way which your Father

would have you pursue, the perplexity vanishes, and trustfully you may follow on. But there is something more. Who was it at that last supper who found out the secrets of the Master's mind as to the traitor? Was it not he who leaned upon His bosom? it was John, who was so near in that sweet resting-place that when the Lord rose the disciple rose also. Ah, beloved of the Lord, you and I are entitled to be there, to rest our head upon His bosom, and in that position of calm and hallowed intimacy to see His eye for our direction down here, and to know the very secrets of His heart of love, to go where He goes, to rest where He rests, to follow where He leads.

But look again at the high priest. We see his head covered with

THE MITRE.

The women were taught to cover their heads in token of subjection; and here we have our High Priest standing with covered brow as subject to God, and subject too on our behalf. He wears the mitre on His head. The head is the seat of the will, the seat of thought, the seat of purpose; and He has us in His thought and in His purpose, and that purpose is, notwithstanding all our failures, to bring us to glory.

Our High Priest bears "*the iniquity*" of our

holy things—all the evil and failure on our part connected with them. Oh, needed, loving provision of our God! There He stands; His brow, as He appears before God, is beheld in its effulgence of divine light and glory, bearing *for us*, through His own merit, the mystic inscription, "HOLINESS TO THE LORD."

That inscription is recorded in gold—precious and enduring substance. It is engraven on a plate or flower of gold—a golden flower never to fade—beautiful on the head of Aaron, placed so conspicuously that he could not be before God, and not have it before His divine, complacent eye. "Holiness to the Lord" for Israel was always there. Like the fire on the altar which was always burning, that no poor sinner could come with a sacrifice and find no fire, no acceptable time; so now, no worshipper, laden with the sins of his holy things, can ever fail to have his need met by that which was always upon the golden plate or flower of the mitre. And, oh, why was it there? Was it merely that their iniquity may be put away? No, indeed, it was that "they," either the holy things themselves or the people whose things they were, "might be accepted." Oh, to know and believe this for ourselves! All our iniquities, the sins of our holy things, gone; our holy things and our-selves *accepted*—accepted in Aaron, "accepted in

the Beloved." What days of sorrow and dejection
of soul would the belief of this save us. Think
how blessed—a God-man between God and us!
none of our iniquities reaching God, each one taken
in hand by Him who is there for us. All that is
of His own creating He presents, while all that is
ours He provides against by ever being in the
presence of God, what indeed we in ourselves are
not, " Holiness to the Lord."

Let me name two points in which, as to holy
things, there is special failure. We fail in our
worship. We fail in our service. As to our
worship, have we never in moments of communion
heard the Lord's voice, but failed in obeying it?
Or have we never professedly breathed desire into
His ear, and soon after, our souls being out of
communion, have we not forgotten our request?
And have we never when in worship, having joy,
love, delight before Him, so forgotten with Whom
we were that our thoughts have gone from Him,
and He has been left *alone* in the place in which
we have worshipped? Ah! little is there of our
worship which, like the fire of the burnt-offering,
ascended upwards with acceptance. But how
much of "iniquity" is consumed by the fire, and,
as mere ashes, goes downwards! All that is not
of God, all that is of *self*, must be burnt up.
When one is singing precious words, and the heart

does not respond, oh, what ashes! The same with our service, doing anything for the approval of self or of others, and not as to the Lord, it will all be burned up, and will not stand in that day. Nothing will stand then but what is of God. For the *sins* of our service, happily, there is this crown, this mitre, on the brow of our High Priest. But for the service, where acceptable, there are special rewards. There are three crowns spoken of—the crown of glory, the crown of righteousness, and the crown of life. The crown of glory is connected with *elders*, and evidently has special reference to those who feed Christ's flock. When the chief Shepherd shall appear they are to "receive a crown of glory that fadeth not away." And there is the crown of life, which is connected in Revelation iii. with martyrdom, with those who are "*faithful unto death*." And then the crown of righteousness for all who *love His appearing*. Each one bears a relation to our life, our affections, and our service. Oh, will you not pray that all our service may be of God? that it may be *His truth*, HIMSELF that we preach —a dying, living, and interceding Saviour, and that salvation is not of works, but by faith, even to him who simply *believeth*, and who takes his stand upon the death and finished work of Jesus, as we sing—

> "I stand upon His merit,
> I know no safer stand."

Sweet is the magnificent display of Aaron in his garments for glory and for beauty, and we would add the display was not confined to the Holy Place. On the evening of the great day of atonement, Aaron came out in them, and blessed the people who had assembled, as we may suppose, an innumerable multitude ; for their special attitude was to look for his coming out. He brought with him inconceivable blessing, saying, " The Lord bless thee and keep thee : the Lord make His face shine upon thee, and be gracious unto thee : the Lord lift up His countenance upon thee, and give thee peace ;" answering to the three Persons in the Godhead. We can conceive the glowing glories and the setting sun of an eastern sky, how that all that he was in—his beautiful raiment would be seen in, and be reflective of, that glow. This was not so much to represent a heavenly scene; he came out to bless Israel where they were, and they were taught to look for him. Not that they would lose the blessing if they were not literally looking; many an aged one or a dying one could not, but their normal attitude was that they should see the sight, and receive the blessing. We at once see that this was not so much what we are looking for, the " I will come again, and receive you unto Myself; that where I am," in the Father's house with the many mansions ; but the coming morning, when He will appear a second time, without sin unto salvation—not to die this time, or to be murdered by His own. He would be clothed with mercies, tender mercies for His own Jacob, whom He loved.   To know the blessedness of it you must read all that the prophets have written, of the joy He promised Himself when He will bring His sons from afar, and His daughters from the ends of the earth.   It is then they will see their High Priest in His garments for glory and for beauty; for to them is the promise, "Thine eyes shall see the King in His beauty."   They shall behold the Lamb in Immanuel's land, which will be as the garden of the Lord, and in the midst of that garden there will be the ivory palaces, and the glorious House of the Lord, whence He will again and again manifest Himself.

> " Sing the full glories of the Lamb !
>   The Lamb that once was slain ;
>   Sing how from heaven He comes again,
>   He comes on earth to reign.
>
> " Sing the full honours of His name,
>   Who lives, but once was dead !
>   His rank, His right, His power proclaim,
>   Redeemer, King, and Head.
>
> " He'll see His seed, prolong His days,
>   His Church with rapture own ;
>   He'll fill creation with His praise,
>   And joys before unknown."

Offerings for the Tabernacle

12

The Offerings

"Give unto the Lord the glory due unto His name: bring an offering, and come before Him: worship the Lord in the beauty of holiness."—1 Chronicles 16:29

WE have already witnessed the scene of these offerings in that outer court by which we entered into the Tabernacle, where, as we have shown, was the altar.

The offerings have a remarkable twofold order in the book of Leviticus. In chapters iv. to vii. the order is (1) the sin-offering; (2) the trespass-offering; (3) the meat-offering; (4) the peace-offering; and (5) the burnt-offering. This is how a sinner finds his way up to God into the very preciousness and blessedness of all that Christ is before God. And though these offerings were for a redeemed Israelite, yet are we reminded of that low estate in which we found ourselves when God first wrought His work on us. Where were we

but down, down in depths of conscious guilt, from
which we never could extricate ourselves ?   Like
one utterly sunk, we had to say, " Out of the
depths have I cried unto Thee, O Lord."   It was
here God met us in His gospel, showing us how
sin had been put away by Christ, and now what a
change, what joy and peace in believing !   For
this we had the sin-offering ; but, lo ! a new discovery—sin that we thought was completely gone
was again seeking to assert its power, and even
bringing us under its control.   What ! converted,
saved, and yet *thus ?*   Then God taught us how,
though sin was no longer *on* us, having been put
on Christ, it was yet *in* us.   There was a law in
the members warring against the law of the mind ;
there was the deadly enemy, the flesh, which lusted
against the Spirit.   But He also taught us the
grand truth of our next offering ; for this we had
the *trespass-offering*, which was for even *actual*
trespass.   What a surprise ! what a sweet relief to
find such provision, that our Divine Offering bore
our *sins* as well as our *sin !*   And now a third stage
in the onward experience of a true child of God,
did he want a life in which trespassing should fade
from out of it ; he needed a power that it should
be so, and here the *meat-offering* met his exact
need.   That offering, a sweet savour of representing
the perfect human life of Christ, that life which

He tells us to copy, saying, "Learn of Me;"
Walk even as I have walked. Is this all?
Certainly not; he now seeks for fellowship with
God, and with His children, and finds it in the
next sacrifice — *the peace-offering.* Peace with
God, the peace of God and also the God of
peace. He brings his offering—that is, he brings
Christ to God, and says, "being justified by faith,
we have peace with God." He is entitled to a
plenitude of peace which we love to repeat—peace
in his conscience, peace with God, the peace of
God, the God of peace—peace in life with all its
vicissitudes, and in death with all its pains—peace
as to the grave, and peace as to the judgment, and
the eternity to be revealed. Looking round upon
this he says, as in the R.V., "being justified by
faith let us have peace;" let us enjoy it. Hence
the offerer, as we shall see, is allowed to feed on
the very offering he brought. He first brought it
to the altar, and so satisfied the throne; then God
allowed him a table to which he could remove the
offering, and invite his friends to participate in the
feast. These are four wonderful steps in divine
truth, mighty in their meaning in Christian life;
but there is something beyond yet; there is that
which crowns all by emphasis, *the sweet ascending*—
the *burnt-offering* which is represented as going
up into the very face of God.

Beautiful word, and assuring to faith, is that spoken by the Lord to His disciples when He said, "For the Father Himself loveth you, because ye have loved Me, and have believed that *I came out from God.*" This is what we have all along been insisting on in these Thoughts of the Tabernacle; blessedly, we believe that He came forth from God, came forth absolutely perfect, fitted for the part He had undertaken in the covenant, which, in the mind of God, was everlasting. It was as one who had thus come, that He was the perfect burnt-offering sacrifice. It was Christ asserting that He was free from all taint of ill, so that He could become an offering and a sacrifice for us. This was God's sure and certain thought from all eternity, and now that in image He is laid upon the altar, the image or the sacrifice must be correspondingly perfect. Hence, over that sacrifice the Father could say, "This is My beloved Son, in whom I am well pleased;" and He could reply, "Lo, I come to do Thy will, O God!" Refreshing to my soul is the sight of Him thus, even the very thought of it brings sweetness to our breasts.

What is this but Christ Himself? Before all worlds, as well as when He appeared, He could say, "I am Thy 'beloved Son'—fitted therefore to undertake the work Thou givest Me to do;" and in

that wonderful perfection will we have an inheritance unspeakable, when perfect in all His perfection,
and accepted in all His acceptance,—these various
aspects of the experience of a child of God, are all
presented to us in these five Tabernacle offerings.

Oh, I have found something inexpressibly
sweet to my own soul in these offerings ; for I
have sin inborn, inbred ; and, secondly, sin, if
allowed, becomes a trespass ; then, if I want the
trespassing to fade away from my life, the meat-
offering, presents for my copying, the perfect life
of Christ : then follows in the peace-offering
communion with God, and in the burnt-offering
sacrifice, I find the very highest conceivable
standing, and life in being accepted in all the
acceptableness of that absolutely perfect One.
Mary was told that she was well favoured of the
Lord, which is the same root as being "accepted
in the Beloved."

These give the real savour of Christ ; how much
they lose who have no intelligent sense of the
applicability thus of Christ, to all our possible
need for our present use in every condition.

Let us refer again to the twofold order. The
burnt-offering stands at the head of all the offerings, as seen by God in Leviticus i. ; whereas in
chapter iv. it is the last enumerated.

In the one case God has found His way to

reach the sinner, beginning from eternity with His perfect Son, who would be quite able to save, and who, in His death on the cross, would prove the salvation of the sinner.

In the other, it is man finding his way up to God; he begins therefore with his sin, and goes on to perfection, finding Christ all that He is to God and has been from everlasting, and his own wonderful place and perfection in Him.

Now in Leviticus i. God's eye is first of all upon His own perfect One, who before all worlds was His delight. It is He who, because of His perfectness, is qualified to undertake a work for the sinful and the lost, and here we find Him presenting Himself to God, and presenting Himself voluntarily, without spot or blemish. But the offerer also presented Him. God had assigned what these burnt-offerings were to be: one was an ox, which told of patient labour; another a lamb, which told of meekness; and the dove, as shewing uncomplaining innocence.

And how available to all! Some were rich, and they could bring a costly ox; others were poorer, and they could bring a sheep or a lamb; but some were very poor, and they could bring a little turtle dove, as did evidently the mother of the infant Child Jesus, who, when she appeared at the dedication, seemingly could only bring two turtle

doves and one young pigeon. These were all
slain outside at the entrance, but were offered
on the altar inside the court. Thus all our needs
are met, not now in these several offerings, but in
the one offering offered once for all, to bear the
sins of many.

And what an encouragement for all to avail
themselves of it! In Leviticus i. it is said, "If
any man bring an offering." Note that little yet
great word "*any*," comprehensive of every soul
throughout the millions of Israel, like our own
sweet "whosoever will" and "him that cometh to
Me I will in no wise cast out." We know not if the
Israelite himself had full understanding of these
offerings, but we have. They were both parable
and prophecy, and have been accomplished in
Christ, so blessedly typified throughout.

Let us now consider

THE BURNT-OFFERING.

"The Lord called unto Moses, and spake unto
him out of the door of the tabernacle of the
congregation." This is where God was. He had
placed Himself there for a purpose ; viz., that His
people whom He had redeemed might not only
approach Him, but have fellowship with Him. At
Sinai, if so much as a beast touch the mountain
it shall be stoned or thrust through with a dart,

but here all is rest and acceptance in God's presence. "It [the sacrifice] shall be accepted for him." Then follows the description how the sacrifice was cleansed, cut in pieces, and finally laid upon the wood which was on the fire upon the altar, whence all went up a burnt-offering; literally, an ascending offering of sweet savour unto God. Whatever was put down on the altar went upward, ascended to Him—the ox, the sheep, and the dove, whatever was offered as a burnt-offering. Christ was called the Lamb of God; hence the lamb had been so distinctly offered through the long generations of Israel morning and evening. There never was a time, as we have seen, when the ground was dry round about the altar; never a time when the value of the lamb was not going up to God.

This offering is, first of all, a manifestation of Christ Himself. The ox is the personification of patient service, calmly, ploddingly going on in the day's labour; it represents the unwearying service of the Lord Jesus, in which He served in all His wonderful journey from the manger to the cross. God says, "Thou art My servant, whom I have chosen;" and He Himself said, "Lo, I come to do Thy will." He came to be the obedient servant; He who "thought it not robbery to be equal with God," condescended to be a servant, to take the place of one able to serve. But the offering may be of the sheep. This brings us at once to Isaiah liii.: "He is brought as a lamb to the slaughter, and as a sheep before her shearers is dumb, so He openeth not His mouth." The sheep gives us the thought of patient endurance, of meekness, both which were in Him. We cannot attempt the full photograph of the Man of Calvary, as seen at Gethsemane or on the cross; or tell out all the lineaments of tenderness, patience, and endurance of that wonderful heart of His; but He could say, "Therefore doth My Father love Me, because I lay down My life."

The turtle dove tells of another feature; viz., His uncomplaining innocence. We are told, "when He was reviled, He reviled not again, when He suffered, He threatened not," this was His character. How shall we speak of it in the glory, when we shall see Him as He is, in all His dove-like gentleness and tenderness? The burnt-offering sacrifice was rather to show Christ's own intrinsic perfectness. The animal was washed in water; if it were the bird, every feather was plucked away, every grain taken from its crop, so that the dove was put down on the altar, as far as could be done, in absolute perfectness.

Oh, ye that hunger after real perfection, here

you have it! Are we not one with Him, and
do we not go into heaven on the ground of what
He is, and what He has done?

We ourselves could never come up to the height
of God's infinite requirements; but placing our
hand upon the Lord Jesus, the value of His
perfectness is put down by God to us.   One
with Him who put sin away we are not only
freed, justified from sin, but are as He is.   We
are members of His body, of His flesh, and of
His bones; when He died we died, when He
was raised we were raised; we are perfect as He
is perfect.

This offering is one of the most important.
All goes up to God—shall I say before the face
of God?   The devil's plan is to heap up all the
ashes before our eyes, but the Lord commanded
that the priest should carry them forth without
the camp: *they* were left in the wilderness, when
the congregation journeyed they were separated
from them.   Give me the gospel of Leviticus i.;
surely we could die on this one glorious offering,
God grant that we may live upon it.

But few think as they might of the *laws* of
these offerings.   There are some specified in
connection with the burnt-offering; they were to
be observed in the offering of the sacrifice that all
might be according to the mind and will of God.

There is a mine of truth in each one. The laws were to be observed by Aaron and by his sons.

First, the fire was never to go out, but to be burning all night. We can see the tented army all quiet at night, spread out before the all-observant eye, and this special fire, with so deep a meaning to His own heart, ever before Him. Suppose a man in one of those tents was exercised for sin or for renewed communion, he could then resolve on the offering, just as we, when under a sense of sin, renew our own use of Christ, which blessedly we can do the moment we sin; and as there never was a time when the fire on the altar was out, so there could never be a moment which was not an accepted time with us. Suggestively, we are now in the night of our own dispensation, and the value of Christ before God ascending for us without ceasing. "He ever liveth to make intercession for us." Am I down here often in sorrow and in ignorance? He is there for me. Am I a backslider? This Man who was once a Man of sorrows is the Man of Intercession; He is the ascending Offering before the face of God, and we are accepted in the Beloved in the very light of His countenance.

This offering is an approach offering not only through the night of this dispensation, but through the night of our lives, of our sorrows, of our perplexities and loneliness, conflicts, temptations, and solitary walking. Sweet in the literal night to know that He sleeps not, but is occupied for us there. Then there is another night coming on for each of us, if the Lord tarry, some spot where these bodies must lie in death. Whilst dying, Jesus lives, and lives for us. How different the night of the wicked, only deepening down to the deeper shades of outer darkness, where there is weeping and wailing and gnashing of teeth. Oh, what a thing it is to have this book in our hands, linking us with God and with Christ, fruit first of the sufferings, and then of the glory to follow!

A further law was, Aaron was to put on his white garb, not the garments for beauty and for glory; it was white he wore inside the veil on the great day of atonement. The white garment shows our perfect Substitute who stands for our imperfect selves. I am not to be living a mere life of introspection, however important self knowledge may be, but with the mind aloft I am to be looking at Him.

Another law, the priest was to take the ashes and put them down in a place beside the altar. Perhaps first that at the altar God might see them. God sees that the work is finished—done. "Done," as I have reminded you, is the last word of Psalm xxii., so the jubilant word in the glory will be "*done.*" When the ashes were placed there, then the priest went to change his garment, and they were carried forth into the wilderness without the camp, into a clean place, reminding us that Christ first of all was consumed on the cross, and then laid in the new tomb of Joseph, in which never man had yet been laid ; and also reminding us, again carried out into the world that all might see the work was *done.*

Next we have

THE MEAT OFFERING

the ingredients of which most preciously manifest the Lord Jesus Christ, showing what He is and what we are to be when perfectly like Him. Although called the meat offering, there was strictly no meat in it. It was to set forth the human life of Christ—Christ as man down here.

The component parts of it were, first, *the fine flour* provided from the best wheat, most carefully prepared ; and not only the best, but the purest and whitest that could be produced.

Then secondly there was *the consecrating oil.* It pervaded all the flour, penetrating every grain of it, and besides being *in* it, the oil was poured *upon* it, showing the wonderful twofold connection with the Holy Spirit and the Lord Jesus Christ, first the indwelling itself, and next the coming down of the Spirit upon Him at His baptism in the Jordan.

Besides the flour and the oil there was the *frankincense*, which was carefully placed upon them both, giving forth its sweet odours, especially when the fire came upon it, showing how God was well pleased, delighting in the Son of His love. When the fire, God's righteousness, was applied to the offering, it produced nothing but what was in the offering. The graces *dwelt* in Him; nothing was added. The fire may create in us what God intended when He said, "What son is he whom the Father chasteneth not?" but with Him it did nothing but bring out the excellencies already and always there.

The fourth element—and there was no oblation without it—was *salt;* therefore it was called a continual offering: the salt preserved it. What was in Him never lost its savour. There might be the appearance of the fine flour, but if no salt, there will be no endurance; as once it may be you were in the full enjoyment of everything, now you feel you have lost all. May God teach us from these ingredients, the fine flour, the oil, the frankincense, and the salt, and these all embodied in us, presented as a sweet-savour offering to the Lord.

What is this offering? I believe all the other offerings have to say to Christ's *death*. There was blood with each of them, but there was no blood here; no pang, no groan of death. There was sorrow and suffering, as shown by the fire, just as when in His life He met with contradiction of sinners against Himself.

But who could describe the perfect manhood of the Lord Jesus Christ? There was never one unguarded moment with *Him*. There was never a moment when self was the object of His life, or the centre of His thoughts. This is what is meant by the evenness of the flour—no inequality, Christ was the fine flour from the very first, even as a Babe. He needed no discipline or sorrow to subdue or soften His spirit: *we* need many afflictions and much discipline to form our character into meekness and submission. Affliction *found* in Him these things, but did not *bring* them. David was a man after God's own heart, yet what a terrible inequality when he became a murderer; and even Paul the apostle needed a thorn in the flesh, lest he should be puffed up. The Lord was without sin, and could say, "the prince of this world cometh, and hath nothing in Me." How different would it be with you and me; we may speak many things in praise of fellow-Christians, yet often with a "*but*"—some unevenness. Christ was born sinless, shapen in holiness, not in iniquity; walking down here, when He was reviled, He reviled not again ; when He suffered, He threatened not. He was led "as a lamb to the slaughter, and as a sheep before her shearers is dumb, so He opened not His mouth." Why are we not more like this? do not dream of perfection any more—this is your model!

Down in the fine flour, permeating it all, was *the oil.* All His will, all His affections, all His motives, all the springs of His action, were pervaded by God ; pervaded by the Holy Spirit. Blessed Lord, why are we not more like Thee? Why is not our will more under the power of the Holy Ghost? Why are our prayers not more the outcome of that secret hidden power of Him, of whom He said, "He shall bring all things to your remembrance?" When I think of what Christianity is, as laid down in Christ, and what, alas! it is so often in Christians, I blush and say, 'How is the crown fallen! how is the gold become dim!' Besides the oil pervading it, there was the oil poured upon it ; I am looking for renewed power of the Holy Ghost, not touching the fact that He dwells within us, both are true. He dwelt within the blessed Lord, yet the Spirit descended on Him in Jordan, and I believe there is something corresponding to this to be looked for in the believer. I do believe in special manifestation of the power of the Spirit, and that prayer can bring it down. You know how on review days, when the cannon have been booming, their reverberations have brought down the riches of the clouds? so when we pray yet more fervently, we touch the clouds of divine grace, and the rain of blessing comes down.

Then *the frankincense*, how sweet to think that you and I are in that, in His sweet acceptance with the Father, the odour ever ascending for us before the face of the Throne! Oh, may God teach us by all this what a model there is for you and me, as though He were saying, 'Be ye perfect, for I am perfect.' Note, in Lev. xxiii. leaven was allowed in connection with this offering—sin in the flesh, on account of which the body must be taken down. Like the plague of leprosy in a house, if it were in a stone it had to be taken out; but if it were the house the whole had to be taken down; so with us, sin is in this house of our body; therefore it must be changed by the coming of the Lord, to be a glorified body.

Think of the practical use of all this. Are we not ashamed of our selfishness, our tempers, our inability to speak for Christ? May God put the lever of truth under us and lift us up. When anything crossing our will happens what is the effect? we are down at once. I don't believe in the truth being known and not practised. Oh that we were more Christ-like, more according to this blessed meat-offering sacrifice! There is a grand gospel suggested to us here. How could One so perfect be forsaken by God? why, if He were not here for our sin? If you are not a Christian hear this good news, this perfect One took the place of a sinner, dying for us; and you, accepting Him because He offered up His perfect life for your imperfect, sinful life, are *saved*.

Whatever the meat-offering was, and surely obviously most precious, it was to be presented on the altar to the Lord, a sweet-smelling savour to Himself. That which had satisfied God was to be given to Aaron and his sons for their food, they were to enjoy what God enjoys. In the eternal heavens God feeds for ever on what the redeemed will ever feed; namely, His own beloved Son, who glorified Him in saving them. There was, as I have said, no death in this sacrifice, and the word atonement is not once mentioned in it; but still there was suffering all through the life, not suffering for atonement, but to bring out His perfectness—suffering for righteousness' sake.

You will observe that the order of the meat-offering in relation to the burnt-offering is beautifully following it. There is no mention of death or atonement in the meat offering, but both are named in the burnt-offering. Many are striving to reach heaven on the meat-offering. This is the

mistake of the Arian, but they have not known
the sin-offering or the burnt-offering. We never
can feed on Christ or be united to Him if we are
not in the value of His death—saved by His
blood. The order is, first the cross, then copying
the life, and then the sweet oil on the life, which is
so beautifully shown by the ingredients—the evenness of the *fine flour*. Now there is no admixture
of evil in His life such as we find in His saints, no
departure from what is beautiful, as there was in
Noah, Jacob, David, Peter, and those disciples who
would have called down fire from heaven. For *Him*
there was no unguarded moment, no unguarded
word, no being taken by surprise. Why, we again
ask, are we not more like Him? why not more
fortified by copying Him? Truly marked was
His unselfishness, looking not upon His own
things, but upon the things of others; He loved
doing good to the poor and helping the needy.
Few there are who see the pure, beautiful humanity
of the Lord Jesus. Think of the lame and the
blind, the deaf and the dumb, the sick and the
dying, the sorrowing and the bereaved; how His
humanity prevailed! Glorious philanthropy! He
went about doing good, when the eye saw Him
it blessed Him. Now this is our model. This is
not the well-to-do Christians paying court to the
mere friendships of other well-to-do Christians;

and this is what should never be lost sight of in considering this meat-offering sacrifice when the human and the divine were equally seen.

Mingled with this sacrifice was also the *salt* that keeps from corruption. God's people are God's salt; but if the salt has lost its savour, wherewith shall the corrupt world be salted?

Then there was the *oil* poured in it and on it, of which we have already spoken.

There were several laws affixed to this offering; first there was to be *no leaven*. Leaven in Scripture is always the type of what is evil: "beware," the Lord said, "of the leaven of the Pharisees." He knew they were hypocrites, men who were carrying their colours falsely. The Lord Jesus was the only One who never had leaven; there is leaven in each of us. I can truly say that all my sins before conversion never gave me so much trouble as the leaven I have found to be *in* me since. Leaven was in the first-fruits which were presented to God. (Lev. xxiii.) If the Lord Jesus Christ could not present me to God unless in myself perfect, He could never have presented me at all. "If we say that we have no sin, we deceive ourselves."

Secondly, there was *no honey* in the meat-offering. Honey signifies the sweetness of mere nature, some people seem naturally religious and

amiable, indeed oftentimes more amiable than
those who are Christians; not that I can understand how any *Christian* could ever uniformly
show the leaven or this natural amiability merely.
None of the sweetness of earth, the smiles and
blandness of those born naturally amiable, will
do instead of a new creation, without which no
man can see the kingdom of God. In the application of all this to ourselves, I would say, in the
first place, it was offered to the Lord, that was
one use. Secondly, Aaron and his sons had the
privilege of living upon it; they were privileged
to take what had been offered to God, and feast
on it; the food restored when they were weary,
and refreshed and revived them amid the toils
of service, and after their journeying in the hot,
sandy desert.

Further, only the anointed ones could take
this. The power of all this is just like the power
of the salt, giving endurance. Could you be
living in the sweet enjoyment of the life of
Christ in daily communion with Him, and at
the same time be indulging in sin, or in infirmities, as men call them? The gospel that comes
in here is that the Lord of glory is the perfect
Offering for a sinner before God; and if there
be one who would like to have part in this salvation, " He hath made Him to be sin for us who

knew no sin, that we might be made the righteousness of God in Him." If He had not been stain-
less and perfect He could not have been offered
as a sin-offering, but would have had to die for
His own sins. Can you imagine the awfulness
of the time when, without a screen between His
holy soul and it, the sin was laid upon Him, and
He cried, "Eloi, Eloi, lama sabachthani"? The
meat-offering represents Christ *without* our sins,
the sin-offering *with* our sins, and He became
the one that we might be like Him in the other.

There are two remarkable features about

THE PEACE-OFFERING

sacrifice. The one relates to the altar, which
represents God; the other to the table, from
which the offerer may feed, and to which he
may invite others, as we might say, "our fellowship is with the Father, and with His Son Jesus
Christ." That which was put on the altar was
typical of Christ, and that put on the table
typified the same. The priest was so to dissect
the sacrifice—the bullock, or the goat, or the
lamb—that he might separate the fat, which was
not to go upon the table; it was wholly for God.
The same also with the blood; it was all for God.
What the Lord Jesus did was to present Himself
to God. But as you cannot take from an animal

its fat without taking its life, so there was no
means of manifesting the full perfections of Christ
but by His death. He became obedient unto
death; "Therefore doth My Father love Me,
because I lay down My life." Whatever Christ
did was in subjection to His Father's will; fat
represents the full energy of the will, as when it is
said, "Jeshurun waxed fat and kicked." The
Lord yielded up His will to God, image of this
was when He could say, "I may tell all My bones:
they look and stare upon Me." But before the
cross in Gethsemane, when His own will would
have caused Him to shrink from the cup, then
He looked up and said, "not My will, but Thine
be done." And He could say, "the cup which
My Father hath given Me, shall I not drink
it?" The only yoke He ever wore was one
of subjection to the will of His Father, He calls
it, "My yoke." His Father would have Him
die, He put Himself into the yoke of that will,
and going with it was sustained by it. The reason
why so many Christians are miserable is, that
there is resistance to this yoke. God wants them
to walk with Him, but they walk with the world:
God says you must copy Christ; they say we
must copy the world. God therefore sends chastise-
ment, there is scarcely a family but has some
trouble or anxiety, and I believe this is the reason:

there is no clear obedience in life or walk. What we want is to be like Caleb, who "followed the Lord fully." "Whosoever abideth in Him sinneth not." If you want a holy life, you must abide in Him in complete subjection. Trouble comes, and a man says, "I would give everything I possess for this not to have happened; anything but this!" And so he goes to his pillow, and cannot sleep; to his table, and cannot eat; a gloom seems to be hanging over him. How different if he said, "My Father sends this trouble; I must company with Him in it!" thus he puts his neck into the yoke, and finds His yoke is easy, and His burden light.

In this peace-offering we have the Lord in all His perfectness. When He was here He said, "I do always those things that please Him;" so that when we see what He did, we know what His Father's will was. Once, outside a village, He met a funeral procession, and gave back to the sorrowing mother her son; this was the Father's will. Then, in the garden of Gethsemane, His Father's will was that He should suffer, He says, "not My will, but Thine be done." In our troubles, sorrows, cares, reverses, are *our* inmost wills thus subject to God? It is often the little worries that do the harm, robbing us of our peace, even more than the great troubles; we put up fences to guard the vines, but they do not keep out the little foxes that spoil the grapes.

The name of this offering indicates its nature ; it is the *peace-offering* sacrifice. The word is plural, as much as to say, when you have Christ you have peace, an accumulation of peace—peace with God, peace in your conscience, peace in life, peace in death, peace under, or rather above, all circumstances; like a river ever flowing, ever fresh. Sweet that word, "Thou wilt keep him in *perfect peace* whose mind is stayed on Thee." Note, not on circumstances, as Peter amongst the waves, but on Thee. Another precious word is this : "Peace, peace"—duplicated peace—"Peace, peace to him that is far off, and to him that is near." If you have Christ thus—this peace—you have all that you want; many Christians with all this wealth unsearchable, which they have in Him, do not use the millionth part of it. Are you using it? are you in the enjoyment of it—peace with God? if not, you must away at once with the sin-offering, or trespass-offering, looking straight up to God—it is the work of a moment—then you will know the blessedness of this offering also.

The blood was on the altar, that satisfied God. The shoulder, the seat of mighty power, and the breast, the seat of the affections, were placed on the table for the use of the offerer. It was not there so much a question of sins, but of communion. The Israelites used this offering whenever they wanted to present any special thanksgiving; and what of us, with Christ, who is our peace? why surely this—

> " Were the whole realm of nature mine
>   That were a present far too small ;
> Love so amazing, so divine,
>   Demands my soul, my life, my all."

We have contemplated the three sweet-savour offerings; the two remaining are

SIN-OFFERINGS,

and not for a sweet savour. The first three, shall I say? satisfied the heart of God, the sin-offerings met the need of the sinner. When man brought the sweet-savour offerings he came as a worshipper in the enjoyment of realized communion with Him ; but when he brought the other, he came as a sinner, as one standing in the light of recent sin. When the offerer put his hand on the sweet-savour offering, it was as if he took to himself all the value ; yea, all the preciousness of the offering. But when he put his open hand on the sin-offering, it was as if he discharged from his soul the guilt that had brought him there. The action in the two offerings is the same, namely, laying on of the hands of the offerer on the offering, only it

The Sin Offering

The Scapegoat

would seem with this difference, in the one case the offerer put down his open hand on the offering to receive, having participation in its acceptance; in the other case the offerer pressed hard with his open hands on the offering, not to receive, but to empty them of all his acknowledged guilt.

And now let us look for a little first at the offering itself, and then at the offerer. What are the features of the offering? First, the animal offered as a sin-offering must be *without blemish*. This teaches us that though the Lord was charged, as sin-offering, with our sin, none of the sin was His own; and hence it is you and I can go to the eternal Throne, and having Him to present before God, say, "Christ is my sin-offering; He is my salvation."

A second feature is, that when the animal was elected, it was brought to the door of the Tabernacle where God was. On the great day of atonement it was God and the offering only, here it is God, the offering and the offerer. What was put on the altar was naked and open before the eyes of God—all was laid on the divine altar.

Thirdly, the animal was brought before the Lord, that the sins might be charged upon it, the offerer laying his hands on the offering.

Fourthly, when the sins were put on the offering, in the presence of God, God and sin could not

together subsist; hence He poured down judgment on the sin, the offering or the offerer must
go from His presence. What a judgment! the
animal is killed before the Lord, the skin torn
from the body, which is laid bare to the fire of
God's judgment. Life is in the blood which is
poured out; not only is it there before God as
atonement, but it is the foundation of worship; the
lost sinner is not only saved, but has at once
become a worshipper. The sacrifice had been
burnt to ashes, there was need of this. *"Finished"*
was the word the Lord uttered on the tree; all our
sin, our sinful nature, self, sin in the flesh, reduced
to ashes, put away. Thus have we calmly and
dispassionately looked at God's sin-offering.

Let us turn for a few minutes to *the offerer*.
'The offerer shall lay his hands upon the head of
the animal,' the sinner fills his hands with his
sin, and puts it on Christ. The sin and trespass-
offerings had to be constantly offered. The offerer
is identifying sin with the offering because one
with it, as Paul says, "I have been crucified with
Christ." The action of the offerer also indicated
his intelligent confession, he did not come blind
as to his condition; but, pressing hard on the
sacrifice, he could say—

> " Believing, I rejoice
> To see the curse remove."

Let me ask, Have you ever settled this question of sin as laid on the Lord Jesus Christ? have you ever confided in His blood for your salvation? can you look fearlessly on to the day of judgment concerning it? How low, how abject a soul may be when brought under a sense of sin! Think of the experience of the writer of Psalm xxxix.; it would seem that all the evils under the sun pressed upon him when God, through His own light, gave him to see himself in that light. As for man, he walks in a vain show—a sorry estimate of his life we have here—disquieted in vain, heaping up riches, not knowing who shall gather them. Note, the iniquities are the chief thing, and could light be more unlike darkness, or day night, or heaven hell, than the joy experienced when he knew that they were all rolled away? Then, though the earthly house may decay, beauty and joy and peace will be uppermost in the soul.

Finally, when the offerer had done all, he was expressly told that all his sins had been put away, four times in this chapter it is said of the sin, "It shall be forgiven him." A great many people go on confessing and confessing, and there it ends; they never seem to get rid of their sin; it is no good to confess unless we take God at His word. Fancy the offerer bringing his sacrifice, and God saying his sins shall be forgiven him, and yet the

sin *still* against him. Or imagine God burning
the animal to ashes, and the man going away just
as he came. No; if we confess our sins, God is
faithful to Himself and to Christ, and "just to
forgive us our sins, and to cleanse us from all
unrighteousness." "By His knowledge shall My
righteous Servant justify many." It is a matter
of absolute forgiveness founded on righteousness,
followed by a practical holiness; for the promise is,
"to cleanse us from all unrighteousness." This
He does in many ways by deadening the power of
sin. How complete is the work, sins gone with
the sacrifice are gone from God and from the
offerer; and God, as it were, adds, They are
gone from My bar, from My mind. "Their sins
and iniquities will I remember no more."

May you and I, beloved child of God, realize
the joy and peace and assurance of taking God
at His word; yea, may we know the joy unspeakable of looking forward to the time when
we shall see Him, when He shall "come without
sin" to be "glorified in His saints, and to be
admired in all them that believe."

The first three, we repeat, are sweet-savour
offerings, the burnt-offering, the meat-offering,
and the peace-offering. The last two, the sin
and trespass-offerings, are sin-offerings, yet there
is a difference. The one is for the sin which

is in us and our sinful nature; the other is for our actual sins and trespasses, which are the fruit of sin. It might be thought that God could have given all these in one; but no: light shines on Christ from each one, and from every detail of each, so that our gaze is met by a fulness of His preciousness and value which otherwise would have escaped our view.

The burnt-offering stands unique among the offerings. God, in view of our salvation, was satisfied with His Son, who came that He might be obedient unto death.

In the meat-offering He is perfect *as Man;* He presents Himself in His humanity as perfect in His life here. The more God saw Him, the more did He behold Him holy, harmless, undefiled, and separate from sinners. Beautiful is the blameless life of a whole-hearted Christian. I have known some such, whose path seemed ever progressing to the perfect day. Yes, there was sin in them they knew, but outwardly their lives were blameless — their memory to me is precious. It is sweet when we see this in one of ourselves, but it all falls infinitely short of this meat-offering—Christ; in all His life, His acts, His thoughts, and His will, He was perfect; the frankincense was poured upon Him; its sweetness went up with acceptance to God.

Next was the peace-offering. Of this offering especially man was allowed to partake; it was called the offering of participation; it shows how man through Christ can have communion with God, and how God's beloved Son is our peace.

Then, fourthly, there was the sin-offering, as if God had said, Now I must show how you can have peace, sin being righteously put away.

And, lastly, the trespass-offering. What did the thief on the cross know about the burnt-offering or the other offerings? what did the jailer at Philippi? How was it with you when you were first awakened? it was not so much of Christ as perfect Son or perfect Man you thought, but *your sins;* they came up before you in dark array, and your first thought was how to be saved; and when you saw your sins laid upon Christ, all was changed, your face was different, you began to sing—

"Happy day, when Jesus washed my sins away;"

but weeks afterwards, it may be, the feeling came back, and you said, I thought my sins were gone, but I never was more inclined to commit my old faults and sins than I am now. Thus practically we soon learn our sinful nature, which is provided for in the sin-offering: Christ condemned sin in the flesh. In God's order He can go no higher up than His perfect Son, He begins there, and then reaches us through Him. *We* begin with our sins merely, then learn more and more of Him, the Sin-Bearer; but there is no end to the height thus to which we may go.

Many Christians seem to go no further than the trespass-offering; others say they have no need of the second. They say we have no more sin in the flesh, forgetting that the Word says, "If we say that we have no sin, we deceive ourselves, and the truth is not in us;" while others find they have so much sin that they think they are not Christians, and are thus kept looking only at the trespass-offering, where we have seen all our sins put away, and that God in the sin-offering has provided for the root of which Paul says, "I see another law in my members warring against the law of my mind." Then what liberty! what freedom from sin legally! and what fitness now for the enjoyment of Christ!

We have seen how this Tabernacle truth shatters to their own nothingness all those systems of error so rife around us, especially one, hoary with age as it is covered with sin, truly a mystery of iniquity. We would add a word with regard to that system before we part with the offerings. For, first, were not these offerings provided by God? would not Aaron have died if he had added or taken one

away, or if in any single iota he had altered them?
What shall we say to all the so-called altars, over
which men are professedly worshipping, with an
offering of their own devising put upon them?
They professedly offer Christ, body, spirit, and
bones, His humanity, and His divinity, and most
monstrous for this their apology is the Supper!
Some believe in transubstantiation. This was not
what the Saviour said, the bread was not to be a
person, but for a remembrance of a Person, and
not worshipped on a so-called altar. Consub-
stantiation is where the bread is not changed, but
the Person of Christ is incorporated; both these
are the conceits of superstition. What is such a
sign of this age is, that so few voices are raised
against them. It was not so when men were burnt
alive for asserting their falsity; nor was it so in
our own lifetime, when the land would often ring
with the sound of protesting truth. There is no
Christ to be offered on an altar now, the altars
have for the present been abrogated, and the
offerings found their end in the one great Offering; these offerings all had an onward look;
though differing one from the other, they all
represented the one Christ.

13

The Tabernacle and the Temple

"A man of sorrows, and acquainted with grief."—Isaiah 53:3

"Worthy is the Lamb that was slain to receive power, and riches, and wisdom, and strength, and honour, and glory, and blessing."—Revelation 5:12

AND now, as a resting-place, let us glance at a few of the differences between the Tabernacle and the Temple. They are not without design. The Tabernacle is Christ displayed as He was in the past—in His Person as suffering Son of Man, His work, His excellence, His offices as High Priest of our profession and Mediator before God. The Temple carries us on to the time of His glory; His sufferings, humiliation, rejection by man, and denial of His kingdom all overpast, and rest, and reign, and people altogether blessed and glorious. Thus there is a difference. The Tabernacle was in the desert, a waste, howling wilderness, where there were no supplies indigenous—neither water nor bread: the people were wholly dependent on God; He sent them bread from heaven to eat, and commanded Moses to strike the rock, and the water flowed. The Temple, on the contrary, was built in the land—a land flowing with milk and honey— the Canaan of promise; it will be in the garden of the Lord, when wilderness days are over, and the King seen in His beauty, and the long looked-for land will be possessed and enjoyed.

Then further, as another difference, in the Tabernacle the mercy-seat was never long stationary, never long at rest, but always, so to speak, in transit, from the first wilderness days to Jericho's walls, reminding us how now especially, as said the apostle, we are "always bearing about in the body the dying of the Lord Jesus." But in the day of the Temple the ark is at rest. "This is My rest *for ever*; here will I dwell." It will be established rest, established glory.

Notice another difference, the Tabernacle was covered with the badgers' skins and rams' skins dyed red, to protect from the storm and rain and all other inclemency of the scene.

If you can conceive of meeting this vast yet lonely procession, the ark being borne along in the foreground or in the midst covered with these skins, you would have asked, "What is it so carried, so guarded?" what mystery would attend it. There was no beauty that you should desire it, it was like the Man of sorrows, who was despised, and we esteemed Him not; but by-and-by He will be seen in His glory. No longer will the ark be covered with the badgers' skins, no longer be carried about or itinerated as the gospel is now, for the very staves will be taken out, and laid up, as it were, in ordinary for ever, like our old men-of-war, now safe in harbour.

In the glory there will be no need, as now, to "*go into all the world*," for the world will be filled with His glory. Do the vast waters of earth's oceans cover their allotted beds? So will it be with the glory of the Lord; it will cover the earth, as those waters cover the sea. The glory will come from the Jerusalem above—His chosen residence in the heavens; from "the high mountain," His residence on earth; from His Church ascending and descending, as on Jacob's ladder.

Another remarkable difference between the Tabernacle and the Temple is, that in the former the only floor was the desert earth. Aaron, even in his garments for glory and for beauty, or in his white robes, in the Most Holy Place, stood on the bare earth. In the Temple the floor was all overlaid with

gold.   When Aaron went into the Tabernacle, passing the altar of burnt-offering and the laver, then
inside, the golden altar broke on his view, and when
in the presence of God in the Most Holy Place, there
was only what was glorious, all above and around.
These told him of heaven and heavenly things;
but casting his eye downward, he was reminded
that, though happy in the knowledge of God, he
was in a wilderness-waste as to supplies, surrounded by its loneliness and desolation.   But
in the Temple, there was not an inch of flooring
that was not gold; in one case there was the
wilderness, with its sorrow and death; in the other,
in the glorious days of the greater than Solomon,
there will be nothing to defile, the people will be
all righteous; there will be no stony heart as now:
it will be quite another dispensation.   Hence, in
Ezekiel xxxvi., God says to Israel, "I will bring
you into your own land . . . a new heart also will
I give you . . . and I will take away the stony
heart out of your flesh."   God has never promised
this to *us;* He gives us a new creation, shows us
that there is a law in our members warring against
the law of the mind, and that when we would do
good, evil is present with us.   In the day of the
glory, the redeemed will have their life and walk
without defilement.

We read how the Lord came to the sorrowing

prophet Jeremiah, and said, "I am going to put Judah into their own land, and Israel shall be saved." And poor Jeremiah listened, and said, "The Lord made my sleep sweet;" for what your eye sees your heart will feel. He *saw* Jerusalem restored, he *felt* his sleep sweet: so let *us* not be troubled at the sorrows of *these* fleeting moments, for here is something to cheer and lift up our hearts. See the prophecies! God lifts the curtain, and what a sight—an earthly sight, not a heavenly one; little boys and girls playing in the streets of Jerusalem, no want there, the Lord dwelling in His holy mountain, uttering His voice from Jerusalem. Oh, why don't we look forward? why don't we have sympathy with God? for there is not a nation that will not be under the flood of benediction from heaven. This is what the Church of God wants, to be lifted out of self and its own little interests into God and eternity: and while Christians are playing, as it were, with a straw, these grand things are going on. Let us open our Bibles and *learn* them there.

In that gorgeous, magnificent Temple, described by Ezekiel, there are some ninety "chambers" embedded in its capacious solid walls. They appear, many of them, to be simple repositories of the richest and holiest treasures connected with the Temple. For therein are laid all the holy garments, those for glory and for beauty, and the others worn in service, by the priests that approach to the Lord. Also, "there shall they lay [deposit] the meat-offering, and the sin-offering, and the trespass-offering," all of which so wondrously represent, in His life and death, the Lord Jesus Christ. What can we say of these "chambers," these treasuries, but that we are reminded of Colossians ii. 3, where it is said, "In Whom (Christ) are hid all the treasures of wisdom and knowledge." But these offerings again themselves are caskets, each containing some one of the unsearchable riches of Christ—precious to behold, blessed to know.

We have been considering some of the differences between the Tabernacle and the Temple, but there was *one* thing common to both—there was *the blood*. The gold could not have saved, there must have been the death of Him who had first His sufferings and then the glory. Oh, it is the blood I would have before me now! it will be before us in heaven. And you, who have been saying, "How can I see the King in His beauty, and live?" the blood first cancels all your guilt, and answers all doubts about sin, and death, and hell, and gives you the full, free, eternal right to the glory to be revealed.

14

Conclusion

"For ye are not come unto the mount that. . .burned with fire, nor unto blackness, and darkness, and tempest. . .but ye are come unto Mount Sion, and unto the city of the living God, the heavenly Jerusalem, and to an innumerable company of angels, to the general assembly and church of the firstborn. . .and to God the Judge of all, and to the spirits of just men made perfect, and to Jesus."—Hebrews 12:18, 22-24

LET us note that these are meditations suited to the presence of God, when the heart is specially occupied with Him and all those things in salvation and redemption so vital to our enjoyment of Him.

It would be interesting to think what sermons, Bible readings, illustrations, allusions, have been drawn from this grand theme—the Tabernacle, a favourite always with young converts, whose minds and affections are fresh and fully appetized for more and more of the truth which is in Jesus;

also with the more venerable student whose teaching is made up of things new and old out of the full treasury of God's Word.

The whole Godhead is enshrined in the Man Christ Jesus. As God in His marvellous essence dwelt through all eternity in His boundless, shoreless space, and just as that wondrous mystic Shekinah in the Holy of Holies, so we read, " It was pleasing to the Father that in Him should all fulness dwell"—in *Him*, the Man Christ Jesus, whose delights were with the sons of men. It will be for a wonder through all eternity that the lowest sunk—and up to this, to look at man as a rule, a godless being—will in the redeemed state be raised to the very highest height, far above all principalities and powers, and every name that is named in heaven or on earth. My soul, oh, my soul, let me dwell on this! for what sovereignty, what an election, what condescension, what wisdom, what love, and at what a price all this is being accomplished! I say *being* accomplished, as we know not what we shall be, for " when Christ, who is our life, shall appear, then shall we also appear with Him in glory."

We understand now what is meant by the saying, "there is no God out of Christ," and worshipping at the shrine of Christ is not, as a Socinian says, idolatry—it is not idolatry, but the worship of the only true God, and Jesus Christ, whom He hath sent.

How infinite His love! And there it is we see what great delights are before us. Ah! then this poor world will be a different world—I mean this veritable earth—the earth restored to its more than Eden glory, and our joys more than those of the unfallen and the innocent; all He intended at the first, of which sin robbed us more than restored. The better Eden will never be lost; the serpent will eat the dust in his own prison-house for ever. The tree of life was in the garden, and here it is again; a river had watered the garden, but here is a river of the water of life flowing in the midst, not a leaf will die, not a flower drop its beauty; there will be no night, no sin, no sorrow, and no death. Some Christians are very earthly, they never seem to have the imbuement of heaven upon them; others are, as it were, so heavenly, thinking principally of getting rid of trouble and sorrow, that they never revel in the glories which are reserved for this earth. What do they know of the Lord implying that He would drink the wine of the kingdom, that He would drink with us anew the fruits of the vine in His Father's kingdom? In that day the kingdom of the Son and the kingdom of the Father will be our glorious inheritance; so that looking along the line of time there is glory, and looking along the line of eternity it is glory.

Meanwhile, whilst we are awaiting these, we may ponder over the real delights which may soon spring up by the Lord's return, or by the Christian's own departure, remembering he should glorify God in his death as well as in his life—"this He" (the Lord) spake, "signifying by what death he" (Peter) "should glorify God." A Christian should pray that he may never doubt or dishonour the Lord in the day of his departure, and he should expect that his life may be fruitful in blessed testimony after it has ceased here. " I will," says the apostle Peter, "that after my departure" (my exodus) "ye may be able to have these things always in remembrance."

And here I would like to say a word on death. Death! a menacing word to an unbeliever, pointing to an insufferable beyond; but to the believer it would seem there is no death. Our Lord speaks of our tasting it, the "exodus," which was a simple going forth. And when the martyr Stephen was in the hands of his merciless enemies, and the stones were beating in his bodily tabernacle, the Lord obviously came to him, not to give him death, but to take him to Himself; and Stephen simply saw Him, and said, not, " Help me, Lord," but, "Lord Jesus, *receive* my spirit." This accords

with St. Paul, who says, to be at home in the body
is to be "absent from the Lord." In fact, it is a
going home; it is to be "present with the Lord."
When we die therefore, as we say, we ought not to
be looking for some dark, impenetrable passage at
some moment in health or in sickness. The Lord
will be as much seen as one come to receive us
as He was by the martyr Stephen. This accords
with what He calls Peter's decease; Peter was to
have a simple going out. Is that death? How
sweet for a child of God to think of it thus, while
lying at the very gate to think of it as that which
simply and only awaits him now! In all this we
may well say, I would "desire to depart and to be
with Christ; which is far better." What we want
for this is love to the Person of Christ and faith
in His Word. "I will come again, and receive you
unto Myself." But the receiving to Himself must be
like a calm, sweet peace of the Holy Place—not a
ripple of sin's waters, not a sign of death's gloom.

Having known Christ in all these relationships
of which we have spoken, now he is to see Him.
Then no more of the application of Christ to his
sins and his trespasses. He will feed upon Him
for ever. He will hunger no more, neither thirst
any more. White raiment will be given whereon
will never be a solitary spot. He will shine forth
as the sun, no more to be eclipsed by the world or

self.   He will see the King in His beauty, and, surmounting all this, ETERNITY will be affixed to every bliss.   The Tabernacle of God will be with men amid the new heavens and earth in that day which is soon coming.

The extraordinary thought which strikes us over and over again in this meditation, and will through all eternity, is, that He should have made *us* sovereign subjects of such great delights.   We have said He left angels just where they were, only they have a new Bible wherein to read Him. Oh, the sweetness of love—His love toward us! May not the Christian even now know something of it as told out so touchingly, with such reality and tenderness, in the Song of Songs?   It was when the distressed bride had been in search for Him, and had wandered separate from Him, that He then said, in the fulness of His love, " Let Me see thy countenance.   Let Me hear thy voice." And more, far beyond this are His words in the same Song, " How fair and how pleasant art thou, O love, for delights."

Nothing more grieves the Spirit of God who is in us, than a low appreciation of what the Lord Jesus Christ is to us.   Think of Him saying, " Let Me see thy countenance, let Me hear thy voice," " How fair and how pleasant art thou, O love, for delights," and our hearts indolent of it!   Any

other lover would long since have left us to our
own way.   But, as we have said, He tells His
Father about us; He takes with Him, inside the
heavenly veil, all the new pardons we need, and
carries out the sweet original priest's office, which
is to be always occupied for us. How patient, how
long-suffering when He awakens us to this.   He
seems like one whom the Song says is far away on
the distant mountains.   The sight awakens desire,
and then He is seen coming over the hills, which
must be nearer, or we should not see them; and
then where is He?   Looking through the lattice-
work, a candidate for nearest communion; for it is
there He says (and how different from far away
on the mountains, where no sound can be heard, or
lineament of His countenance can be seen), "Let
Me see thy countenance, let Me hear thy voice."
I have often thought that among the sweetest
words is when the bride tells Him that He is *her*
Beloved; yet a far sweeter thing, a far higher
attainment, is when the bride says, notwithstanding
all that she is, "I am my *Beloved's*."   Sweet was
the love, her own personal love for the Lord, of
Mary at the sepulchre, and sweet the love of those
who knew Him so well at Bethany; sweet also
that of Peter and John who had such close and
individual dealings with Him; but the love we
shall have by-and-by will go beyond it all.

And, beloved child of God, though we now part from the precious theme, *we* do not part; we shall dwell together in the secret place of the Most High, and abide there "until the day break and the shadows flee away," our one prayer being, "Come, Lord Jesus; come quickly." "And the Spirit and the bride say, Come. And let him that heareth say, Come. And let him that is athirst come: and whosoever will, let him take the water of life freely." Meanwhile, "One thing have I desired of the Lord, that will I seek after; that I may dwell in the house of the Lord all the days of my life, to behold the beauty of the Lord, and to enquire in His temple. For in the time of trouble He shall hide me in His pavilion: in the secret of His tabernacle shall He hide me; He shall set me up upon a rock. And now shall mine head be lifted up above mine enemies round about me: therefore will I offer in His tabernacle sacrifices of joy; I will sing, yea, I will sing praises unto the Lord."

"A HOMELESS Stranger amongst us came
    To this land of death and mourning,
  He walked in a path of sorrow and shame,
    Through insult, and hate, and scorning.

"A Man of sorrow, of toil, and tears,
    An outcast Man and a lonely;
  But He looked on me, and through endless years
    Him must I love, Him only.

" Then from this sad and sorrowful land,
    From this land of tears, He departed ;
  But the light of His eyes, and the touch of His hand,
    Had left me broken-hearted.

" And I clave to Him as He turned His face
    From the land that was mine no longer ;
  The land I had loved in the ancient days,
    Ere I knew the love that was stronger.

" And I would abide where He abode,
    And follow His steps for ever ;
  His people my people, His God my God,
    In the land beyond the river.

" And where He died would I also die,
    Far dearer a grave beside Him
  Than a kingly place amongst living men,
    The place which they denied Him.

" Then afar and afar did I follow Him on,
    To the land where He was going—
  To the depths of glory beyond the sun,
    Where the golden fields were glowing.

" The golden harvest of endless joy—
    The joy he had sown in weeping—
  How can I tell the blest employ,
    The songs of that glorious reaping !

" The recompense sweet, the full reward,
    Which the Lord His God has given ;
  At rest beneath the wings of the Lord,
    At home in the courts of heaven."